BRAVE
HEART

B R A V E
HEART

And don't for a minute let this Book of The Revelation be out of mind. Ponder and meditate on it day and night, making sure you practice everything written in it. Then you'll get where you're going; then you'll succeed. —*Joshua 1:8 MSG*

A L I E N E   T H O M P S O N

info@treasuredministries.com
www.TreasuredMinistries.com

To my husband, Jim

You are the closest thing in this world to the unconditional love of Jesus.

I love you.

CONTENTS

*Corresponding Brave Heart video series and resources for leaders
available online. Visit www.nourishbiblestudyseries.com*

ACKNOWLEDGMENTS

To my family …

My son Justin found a piece of red sea glass on the beach last summer, three weeks after a hurricane hit the North Carolina shores. If you have read *You Belong to the Bridegroom*, you know why sea glass has a special place in my heart. In this study, a woman shares her story to show that, just as broken pieces of sea glass can be vessels of beauty, God takes the broken things of our life and makes them beautiful.

I love this imagery and have become a collector of sea glass treasures tossed on our North Carolina shores. Storms often dredge such treasures from the depths and cast them to the shore. Each piece of sea glass is a treasure, but red sea glass is the rarest treasure of all.

Not so long ago, I walked through a storm of hurricane proportions. I wanted to quit Treasured Ministries. I didn't want to write one more word. But because of my family who loved me despite my imperfections and pointed me to His perfection, I was able to get back up again and move on.

I found my greatest treasure in my family. The unconditional love I share with my husband Jim and my two boys Josh and Justin is my rarest treasure. Three beautiful pieces of spectacular red sea glass.

Through their compassion, I learned more about what real love is—it is giving with no motive attached. This love compels me to continue the work God has given me through Treasured Ministries. With their support, I found the courage to write again. They didn't see my past problems—they saw this potential: Jesus takes the broken things in our life and makes them beautiful.

DISCOVER NOURISH:
A Must-Read Introduction to the Nourish Bible Studies

You matter.

You are designed to make a difference.

The true freedom and confidence you need to make that difference in the world—to become the woman God created you to be—is released only by resting in the love of Jesus.

Jesus' love for women was undeniable. As we walk through the Gospels, we encounter a Savior who reached beyond cultural boundaries to minister to women. He healed women. He defended and protected them. He forgave them. By grace through faith, he gave them the gift of eternal life, setting them on an equal footing with men in his kingdom.

Jesus' behavior toward women was not the norm in Palestine in the years he walked the earth. Rabbis did not teach women then. But Rabbi Jesus did. He taught women the truth about God and about the purpose for which God created them. And his words of truth empowered women to walk in a new way—by faith and not by sight. Through eyes of faith, these women began to see themselves differently than the society around them did. They saw their circumstances differently. They saw God differently. Their lives were never again the same—because their Teacher had spoken truth to them that they would never be able to forget or ignore.

And that has not changed. Today, allowing Jesus to redefine our identity and purpose affects not only our lives but also the lives of those around us. Among his other gifts, Jesus also leads us into a new way of living: walking by faith in him and his words.

We women hear language used by others around us and in popular culture that does not reflect our true identity—and we hear that language all the time. For many years, I allowed those words to define me. And because I allowed others to write my story, I didn't really know who I was. Not until I was forty years old did I understand that any understanding of my true value and my purpose in life must come not from the language of limitation I hear daily, and not even from myself, but rather from the God who created me.

Do you want to gain the courage, confidence, direction, and freedom to become all God created you to be? You can. And God's words—not the words you hear from others, but God's words—are the keys to unlocking this door.

My goal in the Nourish Bible Study Series is to help you gain the courage, the confidence, the direction, and the freedom to become all God created you to be. This series was designed to inspire you to make a difference as you boldly set out on the journey of fulfilling your God-given purpose.

Each volume in the series works similarly:

Each contains this same **introduction**, where you'll discover how to discern God's voice for you personally through the Bible by learning the Nourish Bible Study Method, a valuable tool you can use for a lifetime.

Chapter 1 in each volume lays a strong foundation for your journey by explaining the core concept of that volume's study and providing biblical background for that study's selected book of the Bible.

The remaining chapters of each volume follow a strategic framework. Each chapter was designed to provide a week's worth of daily study. For the first three days of each chapter, by applying the Nourish Bible Study Method to a set of core Scriptures, you will uncover personal truth through the Word. During days 4 to 6, our just-for-women commentary on those core Scriptures will inspire and challenge you to apply this truth in your life, thereby making a difference.

A corresponding video series for each study is available online to enhance your group or individual experience. In addition to the weekly videos, there is also an introductory session that explains how to apply the Nourish Bible Study Method to get the most out of your study. (www.nourishbiblestudyseries.com)

Find support with our resources for leaders including a Nourish Bible Study Series Facilitator's Guide, our Lead Well for Life Change Blog and Podcast, and our Nurture Workshop. (www.nourishbiblestudyseries.com)

Nourish: A Bible Study Method for Life

So let's get started! Let me introduce you to Nourish—the way I and many other women study the Bible, connect with Christ, and receive his truth for our lives.

If this is your first exposure to Nourish, let me explain. Nourish is a proven three-step approach to Bible study designed to help you find truth, confidence, and direction for the life you were created to live.

We all have a purpose—every one of us, male or female. God created us with a plan in mind, and that means every woman is designed to bring value to this world by becoming the woman God created her to be. Imagine how the world would change if every woman were equipped with truth to live out her authentic purpose.

The purpose of Nourish is to connect you with Jesus, the Source of Life, so that you can share this life with others as you live out of your authentic purpose. Without a plan, Bible study can seem overwhelming. It may feel like a religious duty instead of a life-giving experience. The Nourish Bible Study Method can help. Here are the three steps Nourish will lead you through:

- **STEP ONE: Reveal.** Connect with Jesus by studying the Scriptures and allowing the Holy Spirit to reveal truth in those Scriptures.

- **STEP TWO: Respond.** Apply the truth using our IMPACT questions so that your life can impact the lives of those around you.

- **STEP THREE: Renew.** Let the truth you've just learned from God's Word renew your mind. Allow God to anchor his Word in your heart. Putting this life-changing discipline into your daily routine, using our practical method, will change the way you think and live.

Gather at the Table with Jesus

Jesus carved out time in his day to break bread with others. Whether in an intimate setting with his disciples, a wedding celebration at Cana, a seaside fish dinner cooked over a fire with friends, or miraculously feeding thousands with five loaves and two fish, Jesus paused to eat food with those he loved.

Likewise, he made time to share his words with others. Just as food is necessary nourishment for our bodies, his words are essential to nourish our souls: "'Man shall not live on bread alone, but on every word that comes from the mouth of God'" (Matthew 4:4).

Think of your time with Jesus as gathering around a family dinner table he has prepared for you with much love and care. He has life-giving words to share with you. "Every word that comes from the mouth of God" is essential to nourish our souls and give us abundant life.

Think of each step in the Nourish Bible Study Method as an ingredient in a recipe for a nourishing meal. Reveal. Respond. Renew. Each ingredient is important and plays a role. Each ingredient interacts with the others. Combined, they enable you to find and understand life-giving truths in the Word that you've never seen before and nourish your soul for your journey in life.

Let's take a closer look at each of those three steps.

STEP ONE: Reveal

Begin each day's study time by praying and asking God to speak to you through his Word. Then, as you read that day's passage of Scripture, meditate on it, prayerfully reflecting on the verses. Mark the phrases, verses, or words that catch your attention by underlining, highlighting, circling, or writing notes in the margin of your Bible. And journal on your Nourish Notes page any thoughts or questions the passage brings to your mind.

It's important for you to remember that the Nourish Bible Study Method is completely customizable. Nourish provides a framework and a system to improve your study of the Word and encourage personal growth, and then you can shape that system in any number of ways on any given day in response to the prompting of the Holy Spirit and to your own inquisitive mind. For instance, some days I simply mark up the day's passage in my Bible and journal my thoughts. Other days, I feel prompted to learn more about a certain word or verse or to investigate background information on the passage by using outside resources.

Above all, my focus is on following Jesus as he leads me in my search for his nourishment.

LEARN **nourish** FOR LIFE CHANGE

In our free 21-Day Challenge, discover how to use outside resources to dig deeper in your Bible study. (www.nourishbiblestudymethod.com)

STEP TWO: Respond

How do you study the Word in a way that provides the greatest *impact* in your life? By asking the right questions. That approach provides the focus that will help you refine the truth further and apply it more directly and profoundly to your life. That was the purpose we had in mind when we created our six IMPACT questions, listed below.

What happens if, some days, you can't seem to come up with an answer to all six questions? Simple—don't worry about it. If, after thinking about it for a few moments, no answer occurs to you for a question, then move on to the next.

Here are the questions you'll apply:

I.M.P.A.C.T.

Image of God to trust? *Identify an attribute of God, Jesus, or the Holy Spirit to trust.*

Message to share? *Think of a word of encouragement, a truth, or a prayer to share with someone.*

Promise to treasure? *Single out a promise in the Bible to stand on by faith through prayer.*

Action to take? *Think of a specific step God is calling you to take—then take it, if possible, within the next 48 hours. Share the action step with someone for accountability.*

Core authentic identity to embrace? *Identify a truth about how God sees you, then agree with it in your heart.*

Transgression to confess or forgive? *Make a confession to receive healing, help, and restoration through Christ.*

Learn more about each IMPACT question in our free 21-Day Challenge. Discover how and why applying these questions can help you live the truth and make a difference. (www.nourishbiblestudymethod.com)

STEP THREE: Renew

Like a boat tethered to its anchor, God wants our thoughts to remain steadily on his truths. As an anchor secures a vessel so that it ceases to wander, God's Word secures our minds and hearts to him no matter what currents or waves we may face during the day.

During this third step, prayerfully review the weekly Nourish Scripture as well as the journal entries you made during the first two steps. Ask God to identify for you the one anchor of truth he wants you to take away from this passage. An anchor of truth can be one word, truth, or verse that the Holy Spirit emphasizes to you during your time in God's Word.

Record your anchor of truth in the space provided on your Nourish Notes page. And here's an idea: I also record my truth anchor on my phone so I can carry it with me during the day. Be creative. One of my friends puts her anchor on her bathroom mirror so she can't help but see it a few times each day.

In his letter to the Ephesians, Paul encourages the church to "take … the sword of the Spirit, which is the word of God" (6:17). The most powerful way to take your sword with you during the day is to take five minutes in the morning to memorize your anchor truth.

Jesus drew from the Scriptures to defeat Satan's manipulative tactics of temptation so that he could stand firm (Matthew 4:1–11). Similarly, God's Word is our offensive weapon in the battle against the enemy of our soul. Memorization allows us to have direct access to life-changing truths anytime and anywhere.

During the week, keep your mind centered by pressing *pause* periodically to take your thoughts captive and renew them by meditating on your anchor of truth. You may want to incorporate your truth anchor into a prayer. Pausing to reflect on God's Word for two minutes, three times a day, will make a huge difference for you, as it does for me. Besides renewing my mind during the day, I always try to focus on my anchor of truth first thing in the morning and last thing before I go to bed.

I use this anchor of truth daily until the next week, when God reveals another to me in the course of my study.

 Discover additional practical ways to renew your mind with your anchor of truth with our free 21-Day Challenge. (www.nourishbiblestudymethod.com)

Reveal, **Respond**, and **Renew**. Those are the three steps in Nourish, the Bible study method created by Treasured Ministries. Our goal in creating it was to equip you to study God's Word to nourish your soul and unlock the life God created and redeemed you to live. Jesus said, "My **nourishment** comes from doing the will of God, who sent me, and from finishing his work" (John 4:34, NLT, *emphasis mine*).

God's will for us is revealed through his Word. As we respond to the Word and walk out God's will for our lives in faith, the nourishment we receive will flow to others and we will become more and more the women God created us to be.

The table is set and Jesus has invited you. He's ready to dine with you. He has truth to nourish your soul. Come take your seat at his table!

LEARN **nourish** FOR LIFE CHANGE

In addition to our 21-Day Challenge, our website provides further resources for the Nourish Bible Study Method, including our free ebook *Her Nourished Heart*, additional Nourish Notes pages, and sample Nourish Notes pages completed by women just like you. (www.nourishbiblestudymethod.com)

An Option to Consider For a Lighter Load

When you consider the needs of your group and your own schedule, you may decide that you would like a lighter load of weekly personal study. One solution that works well for many women is to simply divide each chapter in half and complete just three "days" of study each week instead of all six. This way, each chapter will take two weeks to complete. That's fine—there's no deadline. Use this method if it helps you and your group create the margin necessary to get the most out of your study without sacrificing any content.

However you choose to use this material, I am so honored you have chosen a study from the Nourish Bible Study Series. For many women, our Nourish Bible Study Method has helped them to allow room for God to speak to them personally each week through his Word. Our prayer is that it will do the same for you!

Chapter 1
BRAVE HEART

DAY 1

There is no fear in love. But perfect love drives out fear.
—1 John 4:18

In her book *Unlikely Loves*, Jennifer Holland shares true stories of animals that have formed an unlikely but deep attachment for each other—animals like an abandoned mallard duck named Fifty Pence and a hunting dog named Skip.

The story of Fifty Pence provides a perfect foundation for our journey through the book of Joshua. You see, the world is a battlefield where brave hearts make a difference. Joshua had to be strong and courageous to lead the Israelites into the Promised Land. You too will need courage and strength beyond yourself in order to fulfill the purpose God has given you.

For many years, I served God with a broken heart instead of a brave heart. When I look at Fifty Pence, I see more than just a duck—I see the heart and soul of a woman. A major part of that woman's story is a God who loves her beyond measure, and a Savior who laid down his life for her, who tied her soul to the love and abundant life that only God can bring. In other words, I see my own story, and the stories of many women I have ministered to through the years.

An Instinct to Cleave

Fifty Pence was a helpless baby duckling abandoned by her momma. Thankfully, a couple saw the precious fluff ball on the street and scooped her up. They rushed her to Annette, a woman known to rescue wildlife.

Annette cared for the duckling. And while she did, she was careful to keep a certain distance so that Fifty Pence wouldn't bond with her. Scientists use the term *filial imprinting* for the natural instinct to form a strong attachment. Soon after hatching, ducklings will follow whatever bigger animal they see first—an instinct that allows them to learn important life skills. If Fifty Pence imprinted on Annette, it would be much more difficult for Annette to release the duck into the wild in adulthood.

Despite Annette's efforts, Fifty Pence's natural instinct to cleave to another won out. Apparently, Fifty Pence had eyes only for Skip, the resident hunting dog. Annette tried to keep them apart for fear that mixing a hunting dog and a duckling might create the perfect storm. To her surprise, Skip began to mother little Fifty Pence, and the two became inseparable. Annette wrote,

> What touched me most was the trust this little duck showed. Here's this tiny, vulnerable thing putting her faith in an animal that might have been her enemy—it's like

going to a lion for affection! I suppose she was lonely and wanted companionship, and normally she'd have had her mother and siblings. So she turned to Skip. And for some reason, this dog with the instinct to attack decided to be loving instead.[1]

A beautiful partnership lasted for weeks between the two mismatched animals. While unlikely, it seemed that Fifty Pence had found in Skip her solution to satisfy her natural, God-given instinct to bond.

Or had she?

One day Annette returned from errands to find that Fifty Pence had flown away. Devastated by her fear that Fifty Pence was not yet mature enough to handle her freedom, Annette searched with great determination for her favorite orphan. Her diligent search stretched into weeks until finally, to her dismay, she accepted that Fifty Pence was gone.

Nor has Annette found Fifty Pence to this day. She doesn't know for sure why this little duck left Skip and her safe haven to venture into the unknown.

But my mind, drawn to clarity, draws my own conclusions. Could it be that, deep down, Fifty Pence's instinct to cleave to her true mother remained? Could it have been this longing that led her away? While Skip the dog was nurturing and provided a connection, Fifty Pence understood instinctively that Skip was *a* connection but not *the* connection— her real mother. The desire for that closer connection won out and gave Fifty Pence the courage to leave the comfort of what was for the allure of what could be.

We Have All Been There

Have you ever felt that way? Felt a longing inside that left you thinking there must be something else in life? In the daily busyness that creates a predictable, mundane rhythm, sometimes that longing is drowned out, but the desire never really leaves you. And at night or early in the morning, when life is still, you still have that childlike faith that, like Fifty Pence, knows you were created for more.

I've been there. The daily rhythm of my life a few years ago was not without God. Church, Bible study, prayer, and serving others were a part of the drumbeat of my weekly life, which I loved dearly. *But the life with Christ that I was exploring through church and Bible study and the life I was actually experiencing were miles apart.* I read about abundant life in Christ, but I was not experiencing it.

And, as with Fifty Pence, an instinct told me there was more to my faith than sitting on a church pew.

Can you relate? You are a Christian, and yet that longing inside you still wonders, *What if there is more to my walk with Christ than I'm experiencing?* Do you want to find the courage and strength to leave *what is* for *what could be* and live life to the fullest? Are you ready to become the woman God created you to be?

That was what I wanted. And that was what I found as I took a journey through the book of Joshua. My relationship with Jesus changed. God's perfect love healed my broken heart and made it brave. You too can find this freedom and live the life you were created to live and give to others.

Ready to JUMP!

OK, deep breath. Here we go. It's time to say good-bye to the wilderness and forge into the Promised Land. Are you ready for the adventure? Yeah, me too.

Today we close with a devotion to keep close to your heart during our journey together. (For a printable version, visit www.boldbraveheart.com.)

Hey, brave heart, I love that you will jump into the unfamiliar. I love that you are bold. I love that you dare to do what I am asking you to do. I love your passion to pioneer (Isaiah 42:16).

So be free to become the beautiful you I have created (Ephesians 2:10).

Let go of what others say and find freedom to walk in your authentic identity in Christ (Galatians 1:10). Let go of every other hand you are holding so you can grab tightly onto mine (Proverbs 29:25).

I am looking for someone whose heart is fully committed to me and not afraid to walk differently by following me completely. Walking outside the world-defined box takes you beyond what is temporary into living for eternal treasures (2 Corinthians 4:14–18).

My presence and my purpose for you do not promise the absence of adversity; rather, they provide the assurance that you will never face adversity alone (Hebrews 13:5). With me, you have a love that will never let you go (Romans 8:38–39).

You see, I need someone to be first (Isaiah 42:16). Yes, I am looking for the pioneering spirit inside you that says, I will not settle for what has always been. I want to uncover what can be. I need you to be the first in your family to walk a different way (1 Peter 1:18–19). I see the generations beyond you who can be blessed. Indeed, my child, I have created you for this time appointed under heaven to leave blessings in your wake as you live for me.

When I formed the world, I did not rest until I'd made a woman, because she was needed to complete my plan. Today I still work to release the God-given potential within women, because they are an important part in a great story written for my glory.

So don't be afraid to jump out of the boat. I created you to be brave! You'll leave ripples of eternal blessings when you walk in courage, trusting in me. Fear is something you learned. Love is what you are wired for, and you'll walk in love when you follow me because I am love.

My dear daughter, if I am for you, who can be against you? (Romans 8:31). My perfect love can cast that fear right out of you (1 John 4:18). Nothing can separate you from my love—and my love is enough.

So walk in that security. If worry walks through the front door, push it back out by casting all your cares on me and trusting me with your whole heart (1 Peter 5:7). And if waves of adversity steal your focus, get your eyes right back on me (Matthew 14:30; Hebrews 12:1–2). Find a promise in my Word and cling to it with all your might (Mark 4:20).

Yes, brave heart, flex your faith muscle. Walk differently by living fully for Christ. You are bold, beautiful, and brave.

DAY 2

Because they have not followed me wholeheartedly, not one of those who were twenty years old or more when they came up out of Egypt will see the land I promised on oath to Abraham, Isaac and Jacob—not one except Caleb son of Jephunneh the Kenizzite and Joshua son of Nun, for they followed the Lord wholeheartedly.
—Numbers 32:11-12

Like Fifty Pence who found herself in a puddle beside the road, where life was not as it should be, the Israelites, God's chosen people, found themselves enslaved in Egypt. God sent Moses to liberate his people from their captivity, much like Annette, who rescued and shepherded little Fifty Pence.

Annette's safe haven gave Fifty Pence a home out of the puddle, but Fifty Pence was not created to live in a backyard attached to a hunting dog named Skip. She was designed for something different.

Similarly, Moses shepherded the Israelites out of Egypt into the comparative safety of the wilderness. But the wilderness was never the final destination God had promised to the Israelites. They too were designed for something more—not slavery in Egypt or wandering in the wilderness but living out their authentic, God-given purpose in their Promised Land.

While in the wilderness, Moses sent out twelve spies, including Joshua and Caleb, to explore the Promised Land and bring back a report to camp. Skim through Numbers 13 and 14 and answer the following questions.

What was the report the spies brought back?

_____

_____

_____

How did ten of the spies respond?

_____

_____

_____

How did Caleb, with Joshua as his silent partner, respond?

_____

_____

_____

How did the people respond?

How did God respond?

Consider the following verses. Why were Joshua and Caleb able to go beyond *exploring* the Promised Land to *experiencing* the Promised Land?

Numbers 14:20–25

Numbers 32:11–12

Caleb and Joshua were more afraid to settle for what was than to pursue what could be. Unfortunately for the Israelites, they listened to the bad report of the ten spies rather than to God's promises, and they reacted in fear. In fact, they actually reasoned that life would be better for them back in bondage in Egypt and sought to stone Caleb and Joshua. The greatest tragedy was that they explored the Promised Land but never experienced it because of unbelief in their hearts. Whatever voice we agree with will grow the loudest in our hearts, and this will ultimately drive our direction.

Caleb's report did not deny the existence of the giants. Rather, he saw the giants in light of the truth of God. This gave Caleb and Joshua courage. Willing to believe differently, they therefore lived differently. They saw their lives through the lens of their knowledge of who God is, and so, trusting God, they pursued the Promised Land with passionate faith. They saw adversity not as an obstacle but as an opportunity to push their purpose forward by trusting in God, with whom *all* things are possible. As a result, God said that Caleb and Joshua had *hearts that wholeheartedly followed him.*

A heart that wholeheartedly follows God: this is our definition of a brave heart. Simply stated, brave hearts believe God, experience the Promised Land, and lead others to do the same. Walking by faith in God and his Word and not necessarily by what she sees, a brave heart finds courage and direction to become the woman God created her to be. Oh, she still feels afraid when adversity arrives. But she understands that her courage and strength come from looking at life through the lens of who God is and believing the voice of truth over the enemies' lies taunting her to fear. Her heart is determined to believe God. In doing so, she invites others to do the same.

This world is a battlefield, and your brave heart is needed.

> For the eyes of the LORD range throughout the earth to strengthen those whose hearts are fully committed to him. (2 Chronicles 16:9)

Much as little Fifty Pence didn't settle but spread her wings in courageous flight to find where she truly belonged, you can take flight to soar into your Promised Land as you journey through the book of Joshua.

Do you hear it, brave heart? It's the voice of your Savior calling to you through his Word. Take his hand and become the woman God created you to be. Life is very safe inside sanctuaries and Bible studies, but you were created to go beyond merely exploring your Promised Land, like ten of the twelve spies. You were meant to *experience* your spiritual inheritance, like Joshua and Caleb. The difference is largely a matter of the heart. This study is designed to help you cross the Jordan and experience the Promised Land step by step as we journey through the book of Joshua.

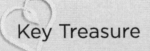

Key Treasure

This world is a battlefield, and your brave heart is needed.

DAY 3

Come to me, all you who are weary and burdened, and I will give you rest.
Take my yoke upon you and learn from me, for I am gentle and humble in heart,
and you will find rest for your souls. For my yoke is easy and my burden is light.
—*Matthew 11:28–30*

We were created to cleave—as Fifty Pence did according to her natural *filial imprinting* instinct but on a much deeper level. God made our hearts that way so we would eventually find him. Our souls naturally crave intimate fellowship with our Creator. And we cannot find the peace and rest we crave until we find him and can rest in him.

Read Hebrews 4:6–13. If Joshua's leading the Israelites into the Promised Land was not the final rest God intended for his people, what do you think our rest, or Promised Land, could be?

_____

_____

_____

Like the Israelites, you have a spiritual inheritance. Our Promised Land is not a physical place like the Israelites' but rather a resting place in Christ: peace with God now and in eternity. Our Promised Land represents the blessings and the grace preached through the gospel of Christ, promised through the New Covenant and purchased through Christ's sacrifice.

True Rest

In the beginning, when God created the earth, he blessed Adam and Eve in a special way. Through their relationship with him, they were connected to the source of life. At rest with God, they walked and talked with him. Then sin entered and broke the intimate fellowship they shared with their Maker. From then on, people were born without that relationship. But God already had a plan to restore people's intimate fellowship with him so they could be tied to him for eternity. And his plan includes you and me.

Imagine that! The Creator of the universe wants to have a personal, intimate relationship with you. God invites you to connect your soul with him not only because he wants to have a relationship with you but also because he is the only one who can fill that empty void in your heart and give you true rest.

Read the two translations of Matthew 11:28–30 below and write down everything you learn from them about what it means to "yoke yourself with Jesus" and experience rest in Christ.

"Come to me, all you who are weary and burdened, and I will give you rest. Take my yoke upon you and learn from me, for I am gentle and humble in heart, and you will find rest for your souls. For my yoke is easy and my burden is light." (NIV)

"Are you tired? Worn out? Burned out on religion? Come to me. Get away with me and you'll recover your life. I'll show you how to take a real rest. Walk with me and work with me—watch how I do it. Learn the unforced rhythms of grace. I won't lay anything heavy or ill-fitting on you. Keep company with me and you'll learn to live freely and lightly." (MSG)

In biblical times, animals, usually oxen, were yoked together to complete a task such as plowing a field. Each yoke was specifically designed and uniquely handmade for a particular pair of animals. There was always a lead ox that was stronger and smarter, and that lead ox would be yoked to a weaker one. The yoke was designed so the stronger ox would carry the weight, and the weaker one would simply follow along to complete the task.

The truth Jesus taught with this picture is as true for us today as it was for the people who heard him speak it in person. He is speaking this to us right now: *Come, take my yoke. Follow me and let me carry the weight. You will find the rest your weary soul has been looking for. My yoke is specifically designed just for you, and when you lay down what you think will give you life, I can bring you an abundant life. The rest I provide is not a rest from problems or the type of rest that the world offers—it is something far greater. You will never be alone. With my strength, I will lead you to accomplish your God-given purpose.*

I love what The Message translation says—"Get away with me and you'll recover your life." Many of the yokes we place on ourselves are self-protective measures that we think will give us life. But they won't. Jesus invites us to lay all that down in order to find real life. If we are honest, we have to admit that the other sources we have depended on to give us peace and rest have not worked. The other ways we have tried in life have left us worn-out, weary, tired.

Jesus Is the Only Answer

Jesus uses another animal parable to explain that he is the only source for real love, life, and rest.

> "I am the gate; whoever enters through me will be saved. They will come in and go out, and find pasture. The thief comes only to steal and kill and destroy; I have come that they may have life, and have it to the full. I am the good shepherd. The good shepherd lays down his life for the sheep. The hired hand is not the shepherd and does not own the sheep. So when he sees the wolf coming, he abandons the sheep and runs away. Then the wolf attacks the flock and scatters it. The man runs away because he is a hired hand and cares nothing for the sheep." (John 10:9–13)

So what is the source for perfect, pure love and real life? There is only one: God. This world offers stuff (wealth, honor, popularity, fun, relationships), but it's always temporary gain. Jesus promises a life that goes way beyond the blessings of this world. Real life. Everlasting and abundant life. We never have to doubt his love for us. He proved his love by laying down his own life. No other love we may experience on earth can compare with this love because Jesus' love is pure and perfect (1 John 4:18). His love is unconditional. An undeserved gift. The Bible tells us not only that God loves us but also that he *is* love and life (1 John 4:8; John 14:6).

Other characters in this story interact with the sheep, but only one of them is worthy for us to tie our souls to: the Good Shepherd. We have other relationships, some good and some maybe not so good, but we should yoke ourselves with only one: Jesus.

There is a thief who comes to kill, steal, and destroy. The enemy of our souls, Satan, is behind all evil in this imperfect world. He seeks to take our hearts captive to other yokes that prevent us from becoming the people God designed us to be.

There are also wolves that attack. I am sure you can remember a time when someone intentionally attacked you verbally, physically, or emotionally. But when Jesus tells us that even the hired man charged with caring for the sheep ended up letting the sheep down, he is letting us know that even though the people charged with taking care of us may be wonderful people, they don't have the ability to give us life.

Only Jesus laid down his life to fight for our hearts, releasing us to live fearlessly for his glory as we look to him as our sole source for life.

People Are Here for Us to Love

Don't get me wrong. We are called to be in community with one another. *But people are not here to give us life—they are here for us to love.* If we look to them for the kind of happiness, peace, and joy that only God can give, we place a burden on them that they simply cannot bear.

What are the ways we might look to people for life instead of loving them? For years, I lived as a people pleaser, seeking my value and worth in what others said about me. Perfectionism was another way I tried to convince the world I had it all together. Other examples of seeking life from those around us:

- Parents who try to live vicariously through the lives of their kids
- Husbands or wives who expect their spouses to make them happy and provide for every aspect of their satisfaction in life
- Pastors who rule with an iron hand because they see the failures of their congregation as an insult

Ultimately, placing our unrealistic demands on people will lead to bitterness and unforgiveness. Why? Because people are imperfect and simply cannot give us what only God can give. Indeed, this points us to a great reality: We cannot love others unconditionally until we see God as our ultimate source for life. We cannot give out what we don't have. God is love, and as we look to him, we can receive his love and give it out to others.

One Name Above Every Name

Just as Joshua was called to lead the Israelites out of the wilderness and into the Promised Land, the Holy Spirit is there to lead you into the life you were created and redeemed to live.

Many scholars believe Joshua illustrates Jesus Christ. Like Joshua, Jesus guides us out of the wilderness and into our Promised Land. Like Joshua, Jesus leads us victoriously through the battles we face in the Promised Land. Like Joshua, Jesus rescues us and identifies us as children of God.

Only Jesus can give us our spiritual inheritance. Moses represents the old covenant—the law. And just as Moses could not take the Israelites into the Promised Land, we cannot earn our way into the Promised Land by keeping the law. It is solely through Jesus Christ that we can receive our spiritual inheritance. "Out of his fullness we have all received grace in place of grace already given. For the law was given through Moses; grace and truth came through Jesus Christ" (John 1:16–17).

In this study, my goal is not to give you a formula or a list of how-tos but simply to reveal Jesus Christ through the book of Joshua. Formulas will only frustrate you. Jesus is the only one who can take you into the Promised Land.

Just like the strong ox takes care of the weaker one, Jesus will take care of you and lead you, taking you to beautiful places of freedom and peace and rest for your soul as you follow him. There, in the loving arms of Jesus, you can become the woman God created and redeemed you to be.

DAY 4

Out of his fullness we have all received grace in place of grace already given.
For the law was given through Moses; grace and truth came through Jesus Christ.
—*John 1:16–17*

If you and I grabbed a cup of coffee and talked long enough, I'm sure we could each share stories about times when, like Fifty Pence abandoned on the roadside, we found ourselves alone, afraid, unsure. We could tell about times when other people's choices—or our own—hurt us. Ours is an imperfect world with imperfect circumstances and imperfect people—and life happens. We would like to control everything and everyone so we won't get hurt. But we can't.

In the past, I tried to fix my broken heart with inner vows, which I viewed as formulas to fix and control my world so I could find freedom, redemption, happiness, and peace. Sadly, all such formulas eventually fail us. Mine did. But in the failing, I found this truth that would ultimately set me free: healing my broken heart could never come from inner vows or rules I keep but from a Redeemer I follow.

False Formulas Cannot Fix a Broken World

In ministering to women over the years, I have found that every woman has a story. Every one has at some point felt abandoned, lonely, afraid, and insecure. Some say, "My mother was so involved in her own emotional trauma, she couldn't begin to nurture me." I've also heard the heartache and tears of women facing a husband's adultery, and of single moms trying to cope because their husbands left the family. Even husbands who provide for their family may be controlling, or abusive, or addicted to pornography or alcohol.

Some women remember a stern and distant father who didn't know how to love a daughter. Others were wounded in the heart by a trusted friend, a bully at school, a teacher or coach, a boss, or even someone in church leadership.

Like Fifty Pence—we're left wondering where we belong. Whether or not we talk about it, the pain inflicted by those relationships is very real. And even years later, the wound may still be raw.

Life Happens

Even with wonderful people around us, life happens. A friend of mine is struggling with the reality that her eighty-year-old mother, who was the loving, steady rock in her life, faces death. My friend is grieving over that imminent loss. Another friend, a young woman from my Bible study class two years ago, feels devastated because after trying for three years to get pregnant, she miscarried. Through tears she pleaded, "Please pray. I am really struggling with my faith." Breast cancer invaded the body of another close friend. Her long journey, while triumphant, was laced with difficult trials.

Life happens in our imperfect world. We bump up against disease and disaster beyond our control, and we ask, "Why, God? Where are you? Have you abandoned me?"

It's natural, as we move into new seasons, to experience changes we may or may not have planned or expected. It's unfamiliar territory. Maybe you've experienced a change recently. You've moved. You lost a job and took a new one—or maybe you're still job hunting and are unsure what to do. Or you may be stepping into the challenges of a new career.

Perhaps you're a newlywed, or you just had your first baby. Or your child recently graduated from high school or got married, and you find yourself with an empty nest. Or you were recently diagnosed with an illness, and now the way you spend your days is changing; you find yourself unable to do simple things you always took for granted. Or a dream you clung to recently died, and you wonder what your purpose in life really is.

Seasons. Some happy, some challenging, some painful.

Trying to Fix It

When life happens, how do we handle it?

Sometimes we create false formulas to handle the hurt. We design our own way to fix things. We build formulas for freedom, happiness, and peace. They vary from person to person, shaped by things like our background, traumatic experiences, family and friends, and the world's influences.

Sometimes we attach ourselves to unhealthy sources for the answers and are wounded as a result. Hurt and needy, we recommence the never-ending cycle of searching for something or someone to satisfy the ache in our soul. But whether unhealthy or healthy, the things or people we depend on for our happiness just don't satisfy—because they are not God.

Our formulas fail us. They create cycles of behavior that become second nature and seep into our subconsciousness. Old hurts create habits that hinder us from giving our hearts fully to God and becoming the women God created us to be.

I know because it happened to me.

My Formula, My Freedom

When I was growing up, like Fifty Pence, I felt abandoned. And although I never articulated it, I designed a formula to live by—inner vows to fix my broken heart and help me find happiness, worth, identity, and ultimately, life. *I will work hard to succeed and thus prove*

I am valuable. If I am weak, I'll get hurt again. I have to be the best. I can never fail. I must please others. If I am not perfect, I am not good.

I became a self-reliant and driven perfectionist. I needed people's affirmation, and when I succeeded, I got it. The world applauds success, and success became my drug of choice, almost a weapon. I was an approval addict who could not say no. I developed codependent relationships. Outside I looked like a confident teenager with titles and accolades, but inside I was terrified. I was alone in my heart, striving to be perfect. I saw failure as unacceptable. At one point the weight of my brokenness became so unbearable that, desperate, I tried to take my own life. That is a scary place to be.

Success is certainly not bad, nor is the encouragement of others. But when these things become our source of life, we are on shaky ground because we place them before God. It's an easy distinction to miss. The source of my affirmation wasn't something bad; it was something good. But good works, when they are not *God* works, can become a yoke of slavery because we have to keep producing them in our own power. Proving myself to solve the shame I felt inside produced pride. My efforts to get my needs met, though well intentioned, were misdirected.

Although I never attempted suicide again, that need to prove myself remained even after I became a Christian at the age of twenty-two. For years, I carried this need into my career, my marriage, my parenting, my ministry, my relationships with others, and even my relationship with God. For a while, on the outside, it appeared that formula was working. However, pride comes before we fall, and my need to prove myself led to a *great* fall. A storm of huge proportions washed away my house built on a false foundation. God in his amazing love allowed me to fall so I could find a far greater antidote than success.

Have you ever had a "sifting season"—a time that reorders your life and changes your perspectives and values? God led me into just such a season to change my source of strength to the only one who could heal my broken heart and redeem the effects of our broken world.

The change did not happen overnight. I had to get out of God's way, and doing so didn't come easily. At first I tried to break free of my habits through sheer willpower rather than leaning on Christ. My shelves were crammed with Christian self-help books; I thought that after reading just one more, and then another, I could reach the freedom we sang about in church. On days when I was "good," I was full of pride and self-righteousness. On days when I blew it, I was filled with condemnation and guilt.

But I lacked the ability to break free from my old formulas, and Jesus never expected me to. All he wanted was for me to take his hand and trust him. Jesus is the only one who can take our broken hearts and make them brave through his perfect love.

I had a decision to make: I could live life on my own terms, fighting my own battles using my formula. Or I could surrender and find my true purpose and identity as a child of God.

I am beyond thankful for that sifting season—a most difficult but beautiful time that shifted me from my formulas to my freedom through the Holy Spirit. When I discovered the difference between following Jesus and following my inner vows, everything changed. Part of this journey was a change in my perspective on God's Word, from approaching it solely for information to seeking Holy Spirit revelation instead. Also, as I looked to God's Word to define me, I no longer needed success to do so. God's Word changed me and continues to change me as I look to the Holy Spirit to lead me.

And that is why I do what I do with Treasured Ministries. I cannot change a woman's circumstances, but I can encourage her to change the direction she looks to find healing. Value. Life. Freedom. How? By inspiring her to look to Jesus as her sole source.

Broken Hearts Are Healed Through Surrender

Brave heart, did you know that when you became a child of God at the moment of salvation, that was just the beginning of your journey? As you follow Jesus, he'll unravel those false formulas that provided no rest for your soul, and lead you to experience the abundant life you were created to live. I myself am still on this beautiful, lifelong journey today, no longer committed to perfection but rather committed to following Jesus.

Complete surrender is the doorway to this life, which comes only from Jesus (Galatians 5:1). Surrender will require the bravest of hearts because you have to walk in ways unfamiliar to your soul. It is impossible to do on your own. But remember from yesterday that you have the Stronger Ox to lead you. All he wants you to do is come to him like a child, depending on him every step of the way. He never expects perfection. He uses your mistakes as stepping-stones as you surrender to him. Through complete surrender, you can do more than *know* about your spiritual inheritance in Christ—you can *experience* it. And in that beautiful place of abundance in your Promised Land, you have the ability to truly give to others.

Freedom is not a destination; rather, it's a journey of living as we are led by the Holy Spirit to become all God created us to be. Where the Spirit of the Lord is, there are liberty and love (2 Corinthians 3:17; 1 John 4:8). In Jesus we live and move and have our being and eternal life (Acts 17:28; John 14:6; 1 John 5:11–12).

We were not created and redeemed to stay in the wilderness. Like the Israelites, we are called to keep in step with the Holy Spirit (Galatians 5:25). We are called to be brave hearts and to walk courageously in love.

Just as it was time for the Israelites to leave the wilderness, it's time for us to understand in greater measure what is holding us back from becoming all God created and redeemed us to be. Our past wilderness seasons should not be allowed to become permanent walls that eclipse the liberty and love that flow from obeying the Holy Spirit.

Ready to move forward into your Promised Land? Don't look back. Take hold of your Joshua—Jesus! Live with impact by letting the Holy Spirit lead you to the liberty and love your heart was designed to experience—and to pass along to others.

DAY 5

You turned my wailing into dancing;
you removed my sackcloth and clothed me with joy.
—*Psalm 30:11*

Put yourself in Joshua's shoes. You were commissioned with this promise from God: "'Be strong and courageous, for you will bring the Israelites into the land I promised them on oath, and I myself will be with you'" (Deuteronomy 31:23). Hoshea, your birth name, means "salvation." Moses changed your name to Joshua, which means "God saves" (Numbers 13:16). Forty years ago, Moses sent you and eleven other spies to survey the Promised Land in Canaan. You saw the enemies to be conquered. Now you gaze across the Jordan River, knowing that it is time for you to lead your people to claim your nation's inheritance.

Sitting in the plains of Moab, you watch your fellow Israelites mourn the death of their first leader, Moses. God used Moses to free the Israelites from four hundred years of slavery in Egypt. You yourself were born into that life of slavery and liberated by the hand of God. You experienced the glory of God as you walked through the parted waters of the Red Sea, escaping the hand of your enemies. Moses was a great leader, and you have had the privilege of being his aide since youth.

Your personal sadness is mixed with fear as you look ahead and take hold of your calling. God called Moses to lead the Israelites out of captivity in Egypt, and now you must lead them out of the wilderness to possess Canaan, the land promised to your forefather Abraham over six hundred years ago.

Read Deuteronomy 34. Moses was a faithful shepherd to the Israelites during those years of wandering in the wilderness, but he would not be the one to lead the Israelites into the Promised Land. Under God's divine direction, Moses commissioned Joshua, his aide, for that task. But before the Israelites could follow Joshua into the Promised Land, there was something very important that God commanded them to do.

What did the Israelites do for thirty days before they started their conquest into the Promised Land? Why do you think this was an important step before they entered the Promised Land?

_____

_____

_____

The Bible tells us that when Moses died, "the people of Israel mourned for Moses on the plains of Moab for thirty days, until the customary period of mourning was over" (Deuteronomy 34:8 NLT).

The mourning period allowed the Israelites to let go of their past relationship with Moses and take hold of the present work God was doing with Joshua. They had a designated season for mourning—with a defined ending. This gave them permission to mourn and yet accountability to move on.

Throughout the Bible, God's people mourned. Much as God designed the Sabbath to give rest to our bodies, he provides mourning as a time of restoration for our souls after a loss. Mourning allows space for our hearts to let go of the hurt and look to Jesus for healing and comfort.

The bravest of hearts give themselves permission to grieve, knowing that this is a part of God's healing process. There's no shame in mourning. It doesn't mean a lack of faith. Mourning is a time set aside to allow God to heal and comfort you. To help you let go and move on to a new season.

Sometimes, for some people, mourning may seem too painful. Instead of using a time of grieving to allow God to heal us, we simply survive. We blame. We bury. We analyze. We deny. We get bitter. We stay busy. We pretend we don't care. I have been there. How about you?

We may have been wounded a long time ago and determined to survive—alone. That may have triggered an inner vow something like this: *I must be strong to protect myself from pain.* We may be so busy trying to be strong and shielding ourselves from grief that we don't give to God what he desires: Our pain. Our burdens. Our weakness. Our needs.

What does mourning mean to you? To me, it requires three essential steps:

- *Acknowledging the hurt*—being honest about my pain and bringing it out into the open where God can begin to heal it.

- *Accepting the loss*—identifying what was lost and taking inventory of the needs the loss created.

- *Accessing the Lord as my source*—taking my needs to the Lord in prayer and trusting *him* to provide. If I don't, I might look to others to fill my needs—people imperfect and limited in their resources—instead of looking to God. He is the only one who can bring true and perfect restoration according to his plan.

It takes the bravest of hearts to grieve. But she who is mighty knows that sometimes we must mourn before we can let go and move on.

What is a loss you've experienced in life that was hard to let go of?

_____

_____

_____

How did you grieve this loss, if at all? If you don't feel that your grieving is done, how can you, over the course of this study, begin or complete that process?

_____

_____

_____

Mourning Will Not Last Forever

Your mourning will not last forever. There will be a time to dance again. After thirty days, grieving was over and it was time for the Israelites to move on.

There is a time for everything, and a season for every activity under heaven: ... a time to mourn and a time to dance. (Ecclesiastes 3:1, 4)

You will dance again, brave heart. One day, God will let you know that it's time for dancing. And one big, brave, beautiful, bold dance step at a time, you will move on by trusting God to make everything beautiful for his glory, in his perfect time (Ecclesiastes 3:11; Psalm 30:11–12).

God promises us that one day in heaven, the mourning will end forever.

He will wipe every tear from their eyes. There will be no more death or mourning or crying or pain, for the old order of things has passed away. (Revelation 21:4)

But for now, while we live in this fallen world, being that tough, self-reliant girl will not bring redemption. Only when we stop trying to survive, and instead run like a weak child into the arms of our mighty God, will we find his resurrection strength, ordained provision, and new, divine guidance.

Go ahead and grieve, brave heart. Acknowledge the hurt, accept the loss, and *access the Lord as your source*. Your heavenly Father, the source from whom *all* blessings flow, delights in seeing you dance again.

DAY 6

As for me and my household, we will serve the LORD.
—*Joshua 24:15*

Often our past experiences prepare our hearts for our Promised Land purpose. Life can be our greatest classroom, as it was for Joshua.

The Lord had been preparing Moses' successor for his calling for many years. Although we cannot pinpoint his age exactly, Joshua was likely at least eighty when he led the Israelites into the Promised Land. In the years prior, he had been a slave in Egypt, a servant to Moses, a spy in Canaan, and an appointed leader of the Israelite army. Delivered from the Egyptians, walking through the parted Red Sea, and defeating the Amalekites, Joshua experienced the power of the living God and saw that he could trust God. Joshua's faith, without any reservations, resulted in many victories for the Israelites in the Promised Land.

However, I believe it was the forty years Joshua spent serving Moses as his aide that prepared his heart the most for his new role. Brave hearts know that in order to be a good leader, they must first learn to follow.

What lessons have you learned serving others? How has a past experience prepared you for your future? How can serving prepare you to lead others?

_____

_____

_____

_____

Servanthood

Serving under Moses for forty years prepared Joshua to become a great leader. Read Mark 10:43 and John 13:12–17. According to Jesus Christ, what must we do to become leaders in the kingdom of God?

_____

_____

_____

Servanthood gives us an opportunity to grow spiritually. It redefines success by measuring it in faithfulness. God calls us to be without pride, and serving others under the direction of Christ (after all, Jesus humbled himself even to death on a cross) moves us toward this goal. When you and I grasp that we are blessed by giving, we come to a place of freedom and surrender (Matthew 20:28).

Trusting God to meet your needs through his amazing love and grace releases you to take your eyes off self and focus on the needs of others. When we stop worrying about who gets the credit and just roll up our sleeves and serve him, we are free to follow him.

Serving in little ways does not require an assigned, official position in Christian ministry but, rather, a position of "Yes, Lord." There is a huge difference. Just because we don't have an official title doesn't mean we are not serving him. When we take the posture of "Yes, Lord," we have passion and purpose in all that we do, no matter the size of the task.

When we accept our role as a servant, we allow God to use us as a channel for his blessing in others' lives. That in turn brings healing to our own lives (Isaiah 58:6–11). Knowing God through his Word is absolutely vital for Christians, but putting God's Word into action is vital to our inner transformation. Thinking that life is all about us and getting our needs met blocks the flow of God in our lives. By serving, we become an open door through which the grace of God can flow. You cannot outgive God. Remember, Jesus said that not until we lose our lives will we find them (Mark 8:35).

Joshua never forgot the meaning of servanthood, even after he became a leader. He continued to speak of himself as a servant of the Lord (Joshua 5:14). Serving God will require you to go outside your comfort zone, which will teach you to depend on him.

Serve Him Anyway

Where is God calling you to serve, brave heart? Are you dealing with challenges, doubts, perhaps fear? Will you be brave enough to serve him anyway?

Serving requires sacrifice. Sweat. Tears. Risk. It requires making ourselves vulnerable. The enemy of our souls resists God's will for our lives; he may cause us to fail and fall, which could result in bruises and bumps along the way. The results our sovereign God desires are not always what we think.

If we're following God, we need to hold on tight to him but only loosely to anything he asks us to build.

Brave hearts find freedom to pursue God's purpose with bold faith by letting go of worldly goals and seeking only heaven's reward.

Courageous faith comes from looking up. A gaze fixed on eternity does not give up.

That is why we never give up. Though our bodies are dying, our spirits are being renewed every day. For our present troubles are small and won't last very long. Yet they produce for us a glory that vastly outweighs them and will last forever! So we don't look at the troubles we can see now; rather, *we fix our gaze on things that cannot be seen. For the things we see now will soon be gone, but the things we cannot see will last forever.* (2 Corinthians 4:16–18 NLT, *emphases mine*)

Paul's heavenly gaze was on eternal goals, building God's kingdom by sharing the gospel. That eternal mindset kept him going even when he faced persecution, shipwreck, hunger, sleepless nights, dark and damp prisons—and death.

When fear has a tight hold on us, it can eclipse our faith in God. Fear and faith play tug-of-war with our hearts. But when we let go of the ropes of such things as worldly success, fear loses its grip, and the force of faith wins. To let go and run with unwavering endurance, look up and seek only heaven's reward.

Redefine success by measuring it in faithfulness. You will find not only freedom but also bravery deep inside you, courage you didn't know existed.

So Today, Wise One …

For that family you are nurturing
    That ministry you are birthing
    Those seeds you are planting
    That promise you are praying
    The friend you are helping …

For that small group you are shepherding
    That dream you are starting
    That marriage you are growing
    That business in which you are investing
    That career you are creating
    That blog you are writing …

Whatever obstacle you are facing … serve him anyway, brave heart. Look up, let go, and serve him. Because as Mother Teresa concluded:

You see, in the final analysis, it is between you and God;
It was never between you and them anyway.[2]

Today when you walk out your door, keep your eyes wide open and look around you. There is a lost world out there that needs Jesus. So take the yoke of the Stronger Ox, walk with confidence into the Promised Land, and make a difference in the lives of others. You were created and redeemed to live in the promises of your spiritual inheritance. Get ready for a beautiful journey of letting go and learning to live in a new direction: the direction of your God-given purpose.

Now is the time for women everywhere to surrender to God and become who he created us to be. Not super-spiritual. Not religious. Rather, women whose hearts are fully surrendered. They are the women God can work with.

Give your heart fully to God and live for his glory, brave heart. Experience a life beyond the dry spiritual wilderness.

Your Promised Land is just around the corner.

Key Treasure

Brave hearts find freedom to pursue God's purpose with bold faith by letting go of worldly goals and seeking only heaven's reward.

Chapter 2
BE STRONG
AND COURAGOUS

Now that we have laid a foundation for our study in Chapter 1, we will shift gears for the remaining chapters of the study. For the first three days of each chapter, by applying the Nourish Bible Study Method to a set of core Scriptures, you will uncover personal truth through the Word. During days 4 to 6, our just-for-women commentary on those core Scriptures will inspire and challenge you to apply this truth to make a difference in your life.

ONWARD!

My nourish notes for Joshua 1

Day 1: Reveal

Meditate on the scriptures, prayerfully reading and reflecting on the verses. Mark the phrases, verses, or words that catch your attention. Journal and learn more as the Lord leads you.

Day 2: Respond

Respond to activate truth in your life. The **IMPACT** acronym provides questions to help you apply the Word. Sometimes you may not have an answer to all six questions.

Image of God to trust? *An attribute of God, Jesus, or the Holy Spirit to trust.*

Message to share? *A word of encouragement, truth, or a prayer to share with others.*

Promise to treasure? *A promise in the Bible to stand on by faith.*

Action to take? *A specific step God is calling you to take.*

Core authentic identity to embrace? *A truth about how God sees you to agree with in your heart.*

Transgression to confess or forgive? *A confession to receive healing, help, and restoration through Christ.*

Day 3: Renew

Carry God's Word with you during the week. Renew your mind daily by focusing on one word, verse, or truth that the Holy Spirit revealed through the Bible. Like an anchor that secures its vessel, renewing your mind with the truth brings security and focus, despite the waves you face during the day.

My Anchor of Truth:

NOURISH JOURNAL

Additional space to record any further thoughts God has shared with me.

DAY 4

Be strong and courageous.
—*Joshua 1:9*

Becoming a brave heart means you will face what you fear. The Israelites lived in the Promised Land because Joshua did not shrink back in fear. Instead, he walked forward with faith in God. He was truly a courageous servant of the Lord. What a great example for all of us to follow. Anyone can sit in a church pew, but God is looking for those women who will follow his voice with their whole hearts.

God told Joshua to "cross the Jordan River into the land I am about to give ... the Israelites. I will give you every place where you set your foot, as I promised Moses ... No one will be able to stand against you all the days of your life. As I was with Moses, so I will be with you; I will never leave you nor forsake you" (Joshua 1:2–3, 5). God gave Joshua a command, then a promise. Joshua was obedient to God's voice because he trusted him.

Although Joshua trusted God, he still felt afraid. In the remaining verses of chapter 1, Joshua hears "be strong and courageous" four times. God also said, "Don't be afraid." It is OK to feel fear when we follow God's voice. In fact, when I hear God's voice asking me to do something, I often get butterflies in my stomach or my heart begins to pound. How about you?

Walk in Faith ... Not Fear

Joshua followed God because he was led by faith in God's promises, not by his own emotions of fear. Being led by the Spirit requires a wholehearted trust in the Lord. When we walk by faith, we surrender to the Holy Spirit's lead and leave the consequences to God. "Trust in the LORD with all your heart, and lean not on your own understanding; in all your ways acknowledge Him, and He shall direct your paths" (Proverbs 3:5–6 NKJV). The more you renew your mind by dwelling on how much God loves you, the more you will trust that his path is best.

I must confess that fear has been a stumbling block in my walk with the Lord. I recently heard God's voice but did not listen because my insecurities gave way to doubt, worry, and fear. As soon as I pulled away from my chosen course of action, I realized I had made a mistake. I thought to myself, *What is the point of being a Christian if I don't follow Christ!* I wonder how many times my insecurities have prevented me from following God with my whole heart.

I have sometimes masked my fear with words like *cautious, careful*, and *dependable*. I am not saying God does not want us to use discernment, but for me, God has revealed that my consistent worry and doubt demonstrate a lack of faith in him. When I fall into worry and fear, I am essentially telling God, "I don't trust you." Often, I have not gone forward with God because I wanted him to lay out the entire plan and tell me everything was going to be smooth sailing. I was so afraid of making a mistake or being out of God's will that I was paralyzed and unable to do anything. My decision to shrink back was actually rooted in my insecurities. Only God is perfect, and he reveals his strength through us as we step out in faith.

I can look back at my life now and see many blessings missed because of insecurity over my past and fear over my future. I guarded my insecure heart from hurt to such an extent that I built a fortress around it, preventing the development of much-needed relationships.

I have worried over my children and tried to prevent them from experiencing any pain. In doing so, I have robbed them of their own growth. Afraid my husband was making a mistake, sometimes I did not respect his decisions, and my behavior chipped away at his confidence. Fear does not affect just you—it hurts those around you as well. If you walk around in fear, don't be surprised when you see fear in your children. I cannot go back and change my past, but I am determined with God's help not to allow fear to steal one more day of my future.

God was counting on Joshua to be courageous. Joshua could have been very insecure—for most of his adult life, he had lived in Moses' shadow, serving as his aide. He was not a highly trained and decorated commander of the Lord's army, only Moses' assistant. The Israelites saw Moses' staff turn the water to blood, part the Red Sea, and make water come from a rock. What did Joshua have to offer? Would the Israelites stand with him?

The Bible says that Joshua was afraid. I would not be surprised if his fear partly stemmed from his own insecurities. God promised Joshua that he would be with him and give him victory, *but it was up to Joshua to replace his fear with faith in his Lord.*

Courage Means Following God

It is the same for us. When God tells us to do something, we can shrink back in fear or we can walk forward in courageous faith. Placing our trust in God can melt our insecurities and enable us to move boldly forward in faith. Courage means following God despite our feelings of fear and insecurity. Our actions can be driven by faith or by fear—it is our choice.

Read Matthew 6:24 and 6:33–34 aloud: "No one can serve two masters; for either he will hate the one and love the other, or else he will be loyal to the one and despise the other. You cannot serve God and mammon … But seek first the kingdom of God and His

2. BE STRONG AND COURAGOUS:
DAY 4

righteousness, and all these things shall be added to you. Therefore do not worry about tomorrow, for tomorrow will worry about its own things" (NKJV).

You are going to serve someone or something. Peace, courage, and freedom from sin come when we serve and fear the Lord alone. Following God is the only sure way. A life lived for God is born out of trust. Security comes from knowing that God loves you and will take care of you. God wants you to fear him only. In other words, God wants you to serve him and follow him and no one else. He told Joshua his success would come from following him alone (Joshua 1:8–9).

Fear is linked with unbelief in God's love for us. Our preoccupation with insecurities from our past and fear of our future can be overcome by knowing God loves us and is for us (Romans 8:31–32). Do you know God is for you? Do you believe down in the depths of your soul that he loves you?

Build on the Past, but Don't Cling to It

Faith is moving beyond the comfort zones of your past. Insecurities will keep you living in the past—faith will move you forward.

Moses led the Israelites for over forty years. At this point, Moses was dead and God had tapped Joshua on the shoulder, telling him to "get ready to cross the Jordan" (Joshua 1:2). It was a new era and God needed a new leader for Israel. Moses had been a shepherd; Joshua was a warrior. Change was getting ready to occur. In this case, the Israelites went with the change, telling Joshua "wherever you send us we will go" (Joshua 1:16). Even if Joshua had not received applause from the Israelites, I believe he still would have followed God's call for his life.

Our insecurities can make us dependent on approval from others. As we move away from our past and our comfort zones to follow God, our friends and family might not approve of our plans or support us. But God calls us to please him, not man. When he calls, we need to follow.

God is always doing something new. It can be uncomfortable doing things differently, following a new leader, or going another direction. If you and I want to surrender completely to God, we must be flexible, faithful followers. Fear keeps us in our past; faith pushes us into the future God has in store for us. Fear of the unknown limits us; faith in the Father allows us to rise to new heights.

Sometimes our past can be a wilderness, and yet we don't want to leave it because it is familiar. God wants to take us outside of our comfort zone to find our Promised Land. What old habit, place, or relationship are you reluctant to release in order to get into your Promised Land?

BRAVE HEART | 49

Suitable ... or God's Best?

Our faith in God means we don't have to settle for "suitable." The Reubenites, Gadites, and half tribe of Manasseh (the Transjordan tribes) made a choice to stay outside of the Promised Land because they thought the land was "suitable." (Numbers 32:1–33). God will never force us to move forward and partake of our spiritual inheritance in Christ. He will never violate our free will. Jesus has opened the door for abundant life; it is our choice whether or not we will follow him.

Perhaps we do not feel worthy enough to receive God's love and so we settle for suitable. Perhaps in our insecurities, we settle for suitable just beyond the Jordan, out of the Promised Land. Perhaps we have decided our ways are better than God's ways. Now hear this: Jesus did not die for you to have suitable. God loves you. He wants what is best for you.

All of us are insecure about something. I have never known anyone who feels completely secure in God. Don't feel bad about having insecurities! They can push you to trust God more. The remedy for fear and insecurity is not more self-esteem, but God-esteem developed by trusting him and coming to better understand how much he loves you and wants the best for you.

Trusting God for Your Future

I wonder what Joshua imagined about his future. Large enemy armies, actual giants, fortified cities with walls that reached the sky, and a river at flood stage awaited Joshua and the Israelites. It would have been easy to imagine the worst about his outcome. It would have been easy to project fear into his future with all the *what-ifs*. This fear could have prevented Joshua from moving forward into his purpose in life. No wonder God reminded Joshua that he would never leave his side.

None of our circumstances are perfect. I don't mean to belittle anything you are currently facing. However, we can spend a lifetime fretting about our future over things we cannot control, or we can believe that God loves us and trust him with our tomorrows. Just as God promised Joshua, God also promises us that he is always right by our side. "'Never will I leave you; never will I forsake you.' So we say with confidence, 'The Lord is my helper; I will not be afraid'" (Hebrews 13:5–6).

> What about your future consumes your thoughts and causes great anxiety in your life? (You are not alone. I still have some worries also!) Write your worries and fears down, and then pray about each one, releasing them to God.

Now that you have released your future worries to God, resolve to yield your thinking to God's goodness and faithfulness. "Do not be anxious about anything, but in every situation, by prayer and petition, with thanksgiving, present your requests to God. And the peace of God, which transcends all understanding, will guard your hearts and your minds in Christ Jesus. Finally, brothers and sisters, whatever is true, whatever is noble, whatever is right, whatever is pure, whatever is lovely, whatever is admirable—if anything is excellent or praiseworthy—think about such things" (Philippians 4:6–8). Remember, God does not expect you to change your thinking on your own; he has given you the Holy Spirit to help you.

I find that it is easy to go back and worry about something that I have already placed in God's hands through prayer. It helps me to say aloud, "I have already prayed about _____ and it is in God's hands. He loves me and is faithful to take care of it in his own perfect way and his own perfect timing. Lord, fill me with your Holy Spirit and help me to let go and trust." It may take only five minutes for me to pick up worry again, and when that happens I pray again. Eventually faith replaces those feelings of worry, and my thinking is consistent with God's faithfulness instead of being consumed with anxiety.

Not even the lilies in the valley are clothed with such splendor as the Lord wants to give you (Matthew 6:28–29). You can trust him with all your tomorrows. God loves us, and when we trust him he can do amazing things for us, even though the answer may not be what or when we are expecting. God's love, if you are willing to believe and accept it, will give you the courage to live your life for him.

Trust in God, Not Yourself

One caution—if your efforts to move away from your insecurities are based on self-reliance, you have swung over to pride. In overcoming his fear, Joshua placed his faith in God, not in himself (Joshua 1:11). Be careful that your courage is not pride in yourself. Your calling is to walk humbly before your God, not to rest in your own strength. There is a subtle difference, but one that matters greatly in the Kingdom. We can be so caught up in avoiding fear by using our own might and self-confidence that we leave fear behind only to reach the other extreme—pride.

What we need is God-confidence. We see both kinds of confidence in David and Goliath. David was sure he would defeat Goliath because he was confident in his God and rested in God's strength—God-confidence. Goliath, giant that he was, was bold and courageous because of his own strength—self-confidence (1 Samuel 17:1–50).

Your ability to turn your insecurities and fears into courage is wrapped up in your willingness to rest in the power of the Almighty and walk humbly before your God. Focusing on heavenly reward instead of temporal earthly reward (Matthew 6:19–21), keeping your eyes upward on Christ, and having faith that God will take care of you will make you a brave warrior for the kingdom of God (Hebrews 12:2).

Where is God calling you to go? What is he calling you to do? Ask him to reveal his love for you. Let go of the past; trust God with your future. And today, rest in his love and know that God is on your side.

DAY 5

God did not give us a spirit of fear but of power and of love and of a sound mind. —2 Timothy 1:7 NKJV

Imagine yourself running a race. Your focus is on the finish line, but along the way you hear voices saying, "You better stop running … you might hurt yourself." Or you hear, "Was it really your idea to run this race?" Or "Don't go any farther—this next leg is too hard for you." "Come down this path. It's the easy way out." Or "I don't think you can trust that the markers you see for the course are correct." Or "I think those people watching you are laughing at you because they don't think you are any good." You can stop, listen to the voices, and quit … or you can choose to finish the race. The enemy cannot steal your salvation, but he will do everything in his power to take you out of the race by tempting you to quit or shrink back in fear.

The race that we are running is to follow Christ. Our eyes should be fixed on him. God told Joshua not to turn to the right or left, but to follow God in order to be successful (Joshua 1:7). Turn to the left or the right in fear, and you are in danger of quitting or becoming distracted from your goal—a life completely surrendered to Christ. The devil is the father of all lies. He uses deception and accusation, tempting you to turn away from God's love and his plan for your life (Genesis 3:1–5; Acts 5:3; Luke 22:3; John 8:44).

Fear That Misleads

Satan will tempt you to fear anything if that fear distracts you from following God. Now, there are certainly natural God-given instincts that protect us. For example, I don't put my hand on a hot stove because I know it will burn me. If I were to throw myself in front of a car and say, "God, you are my protector—now protect me," I would be testing God. The same is true if we choose to live our lives apart from God. I cannot claim Christ as my healer and then indulge in smoking, drugs, and alcohol and expect his protection. The fear that God gives us in our instincts for our protection is different from the fear that keeps us from following God.

The fear I am talking about avoiding is any thought that keeps you from following God. The Bible tells us that this fear is not from God. If the enemy knows you will pull back in fear and insecurity, he can tempt you to disobey God through lies that sow seeds of fear, doubt, and worry.

Read this next Scripture aloud: "God did not give [me] a spirit of fear but of power and of love and of a sound mind" (2 Timothy 1:7 NKJV). The truth behind this Scripture is that fear of serving the Lord is not from God. Do not feel condemned if you feel fear. Do not feel guilty. The enemy wants to stop you from becoming a *brave heart*. Just know that God has not given you the fear, and you don't have to submit to those feelings.

Pull Back the Curtain to Expose Satan's Lies

Think about the scene from the movie *The Wizard of Oz* in which Dorothy, Scarecrow, Tin Man, and the Lion go to visit the Oz. What they see and hear terrifies them. They see a huge face with an evil scowl tinted in green. They see smoke and flashes of light. They hear thunder and lightning. They hear a voice that booms, "Who dares to approach the great and powerful Oz?" But what they see and hear is quite different from reality. Thank goodness for the little dog Toto, who pulled back the curtains and revealed the true Oz. The truth was that the Oz was not a big ugly monster. The Oz was only a small old man, hiding behind a lot of special effects and using fear to keep power over his subjects. Satan works the same way.

When Dorothy, Scarecrow, Tin Man, and Lion discovered the truth about the Oz, they were no longer afraid. It is time for you to pull back the curtains disguising Satan's lies so that you will no longer walk in fear—but you will need more than Toto! The truth in God's Word will set you free from fear. Knowing, believing, and standing on his promises will enable you to pull back the curtain.

God told Joshua to meditate on the law day and night so that he would be successful (Joshua 1:7–8). As Christians, we must stay in God's Word to find truth. Discerning the truth and renewing our minds daily pulls back the curtain and reveals the lies, smoke screens, and special effects the devil has been using to pull us away from the Promised Land.

For example, I used to think it was wrong to enjoy my life. But that's not what the Bible says (John 10:10). I used to pull away from having quiet time with the Lord if I had sinned because I felt condemned. But that's not what the Bible says (1 John 1:9). I used to think I would be happier if I hugged my riches a little closer. But that's not what the Bible says (Luke 6:38). I used to think making everyone happy would make me happy, but that's not what the Bible says (Galatians 1:10). I used to think following God would be confining and dull, but that's not what the Bible says (Luke 9:24). The truth of God's Word has exposed the lies behind my fears and worries, freeing me to put fear behind and step forward to become all God has called me to be.

Name Your Fears

What are some repeated fears that keep you from following God's voice? (I can't do it. I am not good enough. What will people say? What if someone does not like me anymore? I am not sure this is God's will. God does not heal anymore. What about me? If I give this away, I will not have enough for myself. If I wait to hear from God, it will be too late.)

Write down your fears and ask God to help you pull back the curtain by giving you scriptures that reveal the truth. If you need help, use an online resource like www.biblegateway.com or ask your small group leader.

_____

_____

_____

_____

_____

Speak the Word

Every Tuesday morning before I taught a Bible study one spring, Satan threw this at me: "You really do not have anything good to say today." Lies, lies, all lies. I pulled back the curtain by speaking this scripture: "The Spirit of the Lord is on me, because he has anointed me to proclaim good news to the poor" (Luke 4:18). Jesus was actually speaking this scripture about himself, but because I am in Christ, I can say it also! As I spoke these words, faith rose up in me. My fear turned to courage, and I spoke with confidence in God.

God told Joshua to do the same thing. In Joshua 1:8 God told him to meditate on the law day and night. _Meditate_ actually means to mutter or to speak aloud over and over again. Romans 10:17 says that our faith comes by hearing the Word of God. When you hear the Word, faith to follow rises up in you!

The devil tried everything he could to take Jesus away from following God's plan for him to die on the cross for you and me. The devil is a liar and will feed you lies to keep you from being brave. Child of God, you are not to live in fear. Jesus answered the enemy by speaking scriptures aloud to him, and you can too (Matthew 4:1–11). Recognize the source of your fears and pull the curtain back by meditating on God's truth continually. I challenge you to memorize the scriptures you wrote on the previous question. We can count on God's promises—every single one—as we step out in faith to follow him.

Choose Faith over Fear

I bumped into a friend of mine who is a doctor in town. He is known for leading many to Christ right in his office. He is fearless for the gospel of Christ and very outspoken. I asked him, "Hey, what's your secret for not having any fear of sharing Jesus with your patients?" He responded, "It's my faith in God. I have zero fear when I talk to my patients. What's the worst that can happen—they'll get into heaven." The doc has resolved to heal physically and spiritually. His fear is properly placed at the King's feet.

God told Joshua to "be strong and courageous." Faith is the opposite of fear. Fear is not from God. Satan, father of lies, is trying his best to blow smoke. "The voice of truth" tells quite a different story. Whom are you going to believe?

DAY 6

There is no fear in love. But perfect love drives out fear,
because fear has to do with punishment. —*1 John 4:18*

What if you step out in faith and make a mistake? Fear of making a mistake can paralyze
you. In the name of being safe, are you simply standing still? Faith is an action. God does
not want his children to be passive.

Please read the next scripture aloud. "There is no fear in love. But perfect love drives out
fear, because fear has to do with punishment" (1 John 4:18). This scripture teaches me
the truth—that it is OK to step out in faith. God does not tell me that he will love me only if
I am perfect and never make a mistake. This truth sets me free to step out in faith. Why?
Because I know I will always have God's perfect love, regardless of my faults.

God told Joshua that he would be there with him wherever he went (Joshua 1:9). God is
with us always, even when we make mistakes. This is not a ticket to do whatever we want.
God is holy, and it is his desire for us to live for him. This is a revelation: to know that God
gives us the freedom to choose. In our failures, we can grow stronger.

Fear Is Worse than Failure

The more I read my Bible, the more I see that God is not displeased by our failures, but by
our refusal to follow him. In the parable of the talents, a master gave gold to three servants.
Two of the servants multiplied their gold. One of the servants said, "I was afraid and went
out and hid your gold in the ground" (Matthew 25:25). He had a cautious attitude that was
embedded in fear. Listen to what his master said: "You wicked, lazy servant ... throw that
worthless servant outside, into the darkness, where there will be weeping and gnashing
of teeth" (Matthew 25:26, 30). In Revelation 21:8, God lists the cowardly right along with
the sexually immoral, the idolaters, and those who practice magic arts! God would much
rather you step out in faith and fail than sit on the sidelines in fear.

If I miss the mark, the door for forgiveness and repentance is always open. God wants us
to learn from our mistakes. I don't have to fear stepping out in faith because I don't have
any fear of punishment, and I will never lose God's love. Now, God will lovingly discipline
us (Hebrews 12:8; Galatians 6:7–8) so that we learn from our mistakes that carry repercus-
sions. He does that because he loves us and he wants us to succeed. I am told that babies
fall some seven hundred times before they learn how to walk. When they push themselves
up again, they build the muscles in their arms, legs, and core. As their muscles grow stronger, they gain the ability to walk. If they never fall, they will not build the strength to walk.
Falling is essential to walking.

And so it is with our Christian walk. If I fall, I can through Christ pick myself up, make a U-turn, and learn from my mistakes. I have the confidence that God loves me despite my failings and will use every mistake to build me into a stronger servant for him. If I get off the path, God in his love for me will discipline me back on track.

Success is yours despite your mistakes. True success is knowing God's will for your life and doing it. However, you will never have the opportunity to experience true success if you shrink back in fear of failing.

Joshua was a mighty warrior for God, but he still made some mistakes (Joshua 7–9) *However, his mistakes did not prevent him from fulfilling his purpose*: securing the Promised Land for the Israelites.

Seek God's Will

Accepting the fact that we will make mistakes does not mean we throw away the Word of God or stop praying for wisdom. God's Word is a lamp to our feet and a light to our path. I don't wake up and say, "OK, Lord, I want to make a mistake so I can see your glory." No, I meditate on the Word and pray for wisdom because I know, in this crazy world of ours, God's ways are best. God told Joshua that living out the law would make him "prosperous" and "successful." God's precepts are timeless. We are free from the law, but God's Spirit living in us still calls us to holiness. Keep seeking God and praying for wisdom. Christ is the end of the law. Stay closely connected by talking to him often through prayer. Meditate on the Word, yielding to the Holy Spirit as your guide.

Your circumstances will not always line up perfectly with what God wants you to do before you do it. The first time the Israelites crossed a body of water, God parted the Red Sea before they entered the water. The Israelites were fresh out of the bondage of slavery, and God allowed them to see his glory. Of course, when the waters parted, they willingly walked through the divided Red Sea (Exodus 14:21–22). You will see in Joshua chapter 3 that the second time the Israelites crossed a body of water (the Jordan River), the waters did not part until after the priests put their feet in the water. This required the Israelites to walk by faith and not by sight.

Jump!

Faith drives our actions. Although Joshua was probably feeling afraid, he chose to step out. Before we can see God fulfill his promises, we have to step out in faith. Many times, I want God to give me the big blueprint of how it's all going to work out. In other words, I want to see the end of the story and all the details in between—then I'll be bold and courageous for him. Not in God's economy. Often God will wait until after our obedience to give us the tools to get the job done. God calls us to walk by faith and not by sight. Sometimes we just have to jump feet first before God will part our waters.

Where is God asking *you* to jump?

The decision to jump is a choice only you can make. God repeatedly cheered Joshua on, telling him, "Be courageous!" However, Joshua was the one who had to make the decision to jump—and you have to make your own decision to step out in faith in your life. Your pastor, your counselor, your husband, your mother, or your small group leader cannot do it for you.

One summer, my son Josh was on the diving board for the first time. He walked to the edge and looked over to the bottom of the pool. Then he looked back at me with anxiety in his eyes. Mom, Dad, and friends began to cheer him on, but Josh still had to make the decision to jump. And he did! Up to the surface he swam. With a huge smile on his face, he said, "That wasn't scary at all." Back he went, diving off the board for a solid hour! Sometimes we just have to jump before we can see that what was causing us fear never really deserved those emotions at all.

You Don't Have to Be Afraid

Don't let fear keep you from serving God. You don't have to fear making mistakes anymore because God loves you unconditionally.

Commit Matthew 6:24, 33, 35; 2 Timothy 1:7; and 1 John 4:18 to memory. Anytime you are tempted to pull back from doing what God has called you to do, speak these verses out loud and watch your courage soar. Meditate on them day and night if you have to. God wants us to fear him above all. In other words, God does not care if we feel afraid, but he does care if we are passive and fail to follow him. Churches are full of believers, but not every Christian follows God. God wants you to fear him by serving him only.

Your Decision

If you have led a passive life, repent and make the same decision Joshua made to choose faith over fear. Complete surrender to God takes courage. Believing that God will take care of you will give you the courage to follow him. It is simply an issue of trust. Ask God to show you his amazing love for you and you will trust him enough to follow him.

Pull back the curtain to expose the lies from the enemy by staying in the Word. Those lies will tempt you to turn to the right and left, distracting you from following Christ completely. Make a decision to keep your eyes fixed on following your Savior and listen to the voice of truth. The enemy will tempt you to fall away from following God by playing on all your fears and insecurities. Pray and ask God to give you courage. Then choose to walk by faith and not by sight—and jump!

Let's pray

Almighty Father, I come to worship and praise your Holy Name. Father, I thank you that you have not given me a spirit of fear, but of power and love and a sound mind. Reveal any insecurities or fears that have caused me to pull back from doing your will in my life. Show me the truth in your Word. I choose today, with the help of your Holy Spirit, to push forward in faith. Thank you for loving me perfectly, driving out my fear of making mistakes. Help me to remember you will get me back on track when I have failed. I know you love me much too much to keep me out of the Promised Land. God, I praise you that your will for me is to be a mighty warrior for the kingdom of God. Lord, I lay all my tomorrows at your feet because I trust you to take care of me. I confess I have worried so much about my life that I have not surrendered to you. I am through shrinking back. Help me pull back the curtain on the enemy's lies through the power of the Holy Spirit and the promise of your Word. If you are looking for someone who is ready to be bold for you, you have found her. In Jesus' name, I cast out any spirit of fear clouding my view, and I ask the Holy Spirit to fill me with wisdom and courage so that I may follow you for the rest of my days. Amen.

Key Treasure

Make a decision to keep your eyes fixed on following your Savior and listen to the voice of truth.

Chapter 3
RESCUED

My nourish notes for Joshua 2

Day 1: Reveal

Meditate on the scriptures, prayerfully reading and reflecting on the verses. Mark the phrases, verses, or words that catch your attention. Journal and learn more as the Lord leads you.

Day 2: Respond

Respond to activate truth in your life. The **IMPACT** acronym provides questions to help you apply the Word. Sometimes you may not have an answer to all six questions.

Image of God to trust? *An attribute of God, Jesus, or the Holy Spirit to trust.*

Message to share? *A word of encouragement, truth, or a prayer to share with others.*

Promise to treasure? *A promise in the Bible to stand on by faith.*

Action to take? *A specific step God is calling you to take.*

Core authentic identity to embrace? *A truth about how God sees you to agree with in your heart.*

Transgression to confess or forgive? *A confession to receive healing, help, and restoration through Christ.*

Day 3: Renew

Carry God's Word with you during the week. Renew your mind daily by focusing on one word, verse, or truth that the Holy Spirit revealed through the Bible. Like an anchor that secures its vessel, renewing your mind with the truth brings security and focus, despite the waves you face during the day.

My Anchor of Truth:

NOURISH JOURNAL

Additional space to record any further thoughts God has shared with me.

DAY 4

I know that the LORD has given you this land . . .
for the LORD your God is God in heaven above and on the earth below.
—*Joshua 2:9, 11*

What's not to love about the Cinderella story? What's not to love about being rescued by Prince Charming? Beautiful Cinderella is mistreated and stuck in a miserable life serving her stepmother. Day in and day out the wicked stepmother heaps harsh words in Cinderella's ears and an unreasonable workload on her back. However, Cinderella is full of hope. She dreams of a prince who will come and rescue her. Waking each morning, she brings her dreams as seeds of hope into the day and sings, "Someday my prince will come." Well, you know the rest of the story. The prince rescued Cinderella from rags, and she reigned as princess over the kingdom.

From the Ordinary to the Extraordinary

Rahab's story, although true, reads like a Cinderella fairy tale. Rahab was a prostitute making a living at the mercy of her customers. Surrounded by the walls of Jericho, she lived in a culture that esteemed idols instead of the Most High God. Living in paganism, she had no real god to serve. Joshua rescued Rahab from the walls of Jericho, and she lived happily ever after with the Israelites in the Promised Land.

Rahab's life is also remembered in the New Testament. Of all the women involved in the lineage of Christ, God chose to highlight only three—and Rahab is one of those three (Matthew 1:5). In James 2:25, her faith is mentioned along with the faith of Abraham, the father of the Israelite nation. She is also included in the "faith chapter" of Hebrews (11:31).

Rahab's life impacted generations to come, and I believe God wants us to remember what her life illustrates: through Jesus, anyone can accomplish the extraordinary.

Jesus Christ came to rescue you out of the ordinary into the extraordinary. "For if, by the trespass of the one man, death reigned through that one man, how much more will those who receive God's abundant provision of grace and of the gift of righteousness reign in life through the one man, Jesus Christ!" (Romans 5:17).

The name *Joshua* actually means salvation. Many scholars believe that Joshua is an Old Testament picture of Jesus Christ. Now, soak in these words of our Savior: "Very truly I tell you, whoever **believes in me** will do the works I have been doing, and they will do even greater things than these" (John 14:12, emphasis mine). He is talking about extraordinary things!

Jesus Rescues Us

God rescued the Israelites from slavery when they put the lamb's blood on the door. Joshua rescued Rahab when she put the scarlet cord over her window. Jesus rescues us when we put our faith in his shed blood.

Initially at salvation, you apply the blood of Jesus Christ over the window of your heart by confessing Christ as your Savior and putting your faith in the finished work on the cross. The shed blood of Christ rescues you from the penalty of sin, the power of sin, and the dominion of darkness (Colossians 2:8–15).

Jesus' shed blood also completes you to accomplish the extraordinary. Hebrews 13:20–21 says "the blood of the everlasting covenant, make[s] you complete in every good work to do His will" (NKJV). Our weaknesses and failings spiritually, physically, and emotionally are perfected through the blood of Christ. Our brokenness is mended through the blood of Christ.[1] The Bible says we overcome the enemy by the blood of the lamb (Revelation 12:10–11).

You will need to remember all that your rescue means when God calls you to a mission beyond your natural ability. Applying, appropriating, remembering, or pleading the blood of Christ all mean the same thing: remembering your rescue. Pastor Jon Courson of Calvary Chapel writes in his New Testament Commentary: pleading the blood of Christ is not a magic phrase but an "understanding that the victory has already been won, that the price has been paid, that the work of the cross is complete."[2] Communion, prayer, and meditation of Scripture are some of the ways we can renew our minds on our completeness in Christ.

Abundant life is not a promise for perfect people, or for those with a spotless past. It is a promise to those who walk by faith in the finished work of the cross. Jesus supplied us with his blood to rescue us when he went to the cross. The question is, have you applied it?

Faith Makes All Things Possible

Being able to accomplish extraordinary things for God is not dependent on your background. Rahab's life illustrates this truth. Hebrews chapter 11 highlights people who "by faith" lived extraordinary lives to the glory of God. Rahab and Sarah are the only women mentioned by name.

Rahab's background was not prestigious, especially when held to the light of someone like Sarah, Abraham's wife. Sarah was the mother of God's chosen people; Rahab was a prostitute from Jericho. Sarah's direct encounters with God encouraged her to follow the one true God; Rahab's culture surrounded her with the confusion and empty promises of pagan idolatry. Two different worlds, two different lives ... and yet God used both of them to do the extraordinary. Rahab and Sarah had different backgrounds, different cultures, different social standings—but the same faith in God.

Rahab's background did not include formal teaching about God, but she heard the testimony of God's power and might through news about the Israelites' deliverance from Egypt and their defeat of their enemies, the Amorites. Learning about God's power changed her life. By faith, she responded with a heart that wanted more than anything to align herself and her family with the living God.

God Does Not Show Partiality

Romans 2:11 says that God does not show favoritism. He does not show any partiality. He does not care about your pedigree, your performance, your parents, what part of the neighborhood you come from, what church you grew up in, or how many degrees you have. He is looking at your heart. "For the eyes of the LORD range throughout the earth to strengthen those whose hearts are fully committed to him" (2 Chronicles 16:9). When we place our faith in the shed blood of Christ, we are redeemed to reign in life as his ambassadors.

Clearly, the Lord's providence brought the Israelite spies to Rahab's home. I wonder if her mouth dropped open in astonishment when she saw the Israelites standing there. Rahab could have closed the door in their faces, not allowing them or the blessings they would bring to enter her life. She could have said, "I am a harlot, a nobody. I am not from God's chosen people—what do these Israelites want with me? I just don't believe anything good can come from this." But she didn't. By faith, she chose to open the door, hide the spies, and tie the scarlet cord in her window.

Are You Closing the Door on Blessings God Has for You?

What holds you back from believing you are worthy of God's love and favor in your life? What blessings have come your way only for you to close the door because you did not feel worthy? Is salvation a gift from God you have yet to open?

_____

_____

_____

_____

It takes faith in the gospel of Jesus Christ to receive grace—God's unearned favor. God has so much in store for you. God loves you, even with all of your imperfections and weaknesses. His grace is sufficient (2 Corinthians 12:9–10). Open the door! God's love is unconditional.

Fix Your Eyes on Jesus

If I fix my eyes on my imperfections or my circumstances, I feel discouraged. However, if my eyes are fixed on Christ and the righteousness I have through him, I move beyond my feelings into the realm of faith.

There is a sweet security in knowing that God loves you and believes in you. The more you meditate on scriptures that speak of who you are in Christ, the more faith will rise up in you to walk worthy of your calling. The level at which you experience Christ is directly proportional to the depth of your faith (Matthew 9:28–29) because your faith drives your actions (James 2:26).

For a long time I wanted to believe that God's acceptance was based on my actions ... that I had to earn his favor. For example, I wanted to *be* acceptable before I *believed* that I was acceptable. When I began to believe I was acceptable by his grace alone, my actions started lining up with that truth.

Rahab's faith in God drove her to hide the spies, an act that took her life into the extraordinary. Do you have faith in God's love for you? Do you believe you are clothed in the righteousness of Christ? Do you believe God has good plans for you?

God has said it. The question is ... do you believe it?

Will You Please Pray with Me?

God, I thank you for choosing me to be your child (John 1:12), your ambassador (2 Corinthians 5:20), and your princess (Galatians 4:7; 1 Peter 2:9). Father, I praise you because I am in right standing with you (Galatians 2:21). Thank you for loving me unconditionally (John 3:16; 1 John 3:1) and showing your power in all my weaknesses (2 Corinthians 9–10). I thank you for your grace (Ephesians 1:7) and your favor (Acts 2:47) that surround me. You have a plan and purpose for my life. Thank you, God, for your resurrection power living on the inside of me (Ephesians 1:19–20). I praise you for being my healer (Matthew 8:17) and my restorer (Psalm 23:3). You are for me (Romans 8:31), and I can overcome because Christ overcame (1 John 5:4). I am redeemed (1 Peter 1:18). I was created for your glory (Ephesians 2:10). I am a new creation (2 Corinthians 5:17). You take all the bad and turn it for good. I will no longer perform for your love ... I am ready to receive it through your grace! Thank you that by the grace of Jesus Christ, you have crowned me to live for you (Romans 5:17).

DAY 5

Yet to all who received him, to those who believed in his name,
he gave the right to become children of God. —*John 1:12*

Now you are no longer a slave but God's own child. And since you are his child,
God has made you his heir. —*Galatians 4:7 NLT*

Rahab was surrounded by the walls of Jericho. However, no walls could keep her from her destiny. Rahab saw beyond her walls. She looked to the living God to help her, not because she thought she had earned his help, but because she had faith in him, and in his love and power. When she put the scarlet cord in her window, she identified herself as one of God's chosen people and was rescued by Joshua to live among the Israelites.

Explore Your Dreams

Rahab had dreams as all of us do. I believe God puts those dreams in our hearts so that we may fulfill our God-given destiny. We are all divine creations, masterpieces tailor-made to accomplish God's plan in our lives (Ephesians 2:10).

> If you had unlimited time, money, resources, and talent, what would you do to bring God glory?

Self-Built Walls

Even though we are not living behind Jericho's walls, I believe we build our own walls of limitations. Instead of seeing ourselves through spiritual eyes and stepping out to become all God created us to be, we sometimes choose to live a life defined by the world's labels and boundaries. We see our past or our own human limitations as walls that keep us from living out our dreams.

What self-imposed limitations prevent you from believing that ALL things are possible with God?

We serve the one true living God, and you are his child. Dream big. You serve a big God! The scarlet cord identified Rahab as one of God's chosen people. The blood of Jesus Christ identifies us as God's children.

God can and wants to empower his children to do great things for him. Don't live like a hostage trapped inside self-built walls. Open your spiritual eyes wide to see beyond the walls in your life and step out in faith. Our God is bigger than any boundary, and you are his child. Your security, your happiness, and your fulfillment are not defined by your circumstances, but by your identity in Christ.

Discovering Your Identity

What is your identity? You will never be content until you see yourself as the person God created you to be.

Some see their identity in their titles: "I am a mother ... I am a wife." Others see their identity in what they do: "I am a nurse [or a lawyer or homeroom mom]." Others allow their families to define them: "I am the daughter of a successful businessman. I am the daughter of a workaholic. I am the daughter of a pastor." Some allow their past to define them: "I am an alcoholic. I am a divorcee." Still others allow their flaws to define them: "I am quiet. I can't cook. I can't write. I can't speak. I can't lead a small group. I am a failure. I am slow. I am impatient."

Stop! When you received Christ as your Savior, your identity forever changed. You became a child of God.

For many years as a Christian, I suffered from an identity crisis. I allowed labels to define me, and so I lived as an orphan instead of a child. I was not being true to the real me that God so fearfully and wonderfully made. The moment I began to believe I was God's child, everything changed. The focus moved off me and onto Christ.

Time to Let Go

What negative patterns developed by your upbringing are you continuing to hang on to? Maybe you came from a culture of complainers. Is there a root of bitterness or impatience? Maybe you are living with fear, insecurities, or depression.

Rahab let go of her past culture to embrace her future with God. Rahab let go of her past and embraced her new identity as one of God's chosen people.

If you are born again, you are God's child. The Bible says you are redeemed by the blood of Jesus "from the empty way of life handed down to you from your ancestors" (1 Peter 1:18–19). When we become Christians, we have power through the blood of Jesus to let go of old habits of the flesh and pass down a legacy of the Spirit to our children (Galatians 5:16–26). Remember, the scarlet cord saved not only Rahab, but also her family.

Even if your earthly father loved and affirmed you in every way, only by becoming a child of God through Jesus Christ are you made complete. The old you died and Christ now lives in you. You are now in his bloodline. The scarlet cord in the window identified Rahab as "one of them." The blood of Jesus Christ identifies you as a member of the family of God. The more you believe in your birthright, the more you will walk as a child of God.

We Can't, but God Can

Looking beyond the walls of our own human limitations allows us to see that nothing is impossible with God. Do you think that your lack of time, talent, or finances will keep you from following your dreams? Says who? All of us are small and weak in many ways, but God is big enough and strong enough to take our dreams and give them wings. Attempting something we cannot naturally do forces us to depend on God. That's why Paul said that he boasted in all his weaknesses, because the power of Christ rested on him (2 Corinthians 12:10).

You can accomplish anything with God by your side.

As God's children, we can do great things for his kingdom. Millions of people out there are looking for answers that the world cannot give. Jesus Christ is the one who changes lives, rescues, and redeems. Do you want to feed hungry children, minister to abused women, or spread the gospel to the far ends of the earth? God can—and wants—to do all things through you. You have so much on the inside of you as a child of God. If you are God's child, your weakness cannot hold you back … only your unbelief in God's grace can.

Be Willing to Break Tradition

Past traditions can restrict our walk with God. "The women in our family have always stayed at home so I must stay at home." Or "The women in our family have always worked outside of the home so I must work." God calls us to be led by the Spirit, not by our past. If you are led by past traditions, how can God ever bring you into the future?

Listen to what Jesus said to the Pharisees: "You have let go of the commands of God and are holding on to human traditions" (Mark 7:8). There is nothing wrong with traditions unless they limit your faith.

I was once taught that when Jesus was on earth, he healed to prove his deity; but now that he has been glorified, his miracles, for the most part, have ceased. This theory formed a wall that limited my prayers and faith. When I began to take God at his word, I realized that he is the same yesterday, today, and forever (Hebrews 13:8). My prayers changed because my faith gave me freedom to believe Christ above tradition.

Labels

Maybe you live behind a label someone once gave you. We have a tendency to remember and believe what others have said about us instead of seeing ourselves as the person God says we are. Perhaps a parent, teacher, coach, boss, or even your husband once labeled you as incapable, incompetent, ungrateful, ugly, or unworthy. The label has colored your view of yourself, and so you live up (or down) to it.

Remember this: When you become God's child, old labels pass away and you become a new creation. Even if you are already a Christian, perhaps as recently as last week someone stuck a new negative label on you. You are God's child—and that negative label cannot stick to you without your permission.

Perhaps you are the one speaking critically about yourself. Maybe you did something you are ashamed of and affixed a "failure" sign to your forehead. Do not insult God's divine creation! Satan does a great job of condemning us; we don't need to give him any help. We need to leave behind condemning words contrary to what God has spoken over us and see ourselves in the light of his truth.

Let me give you some of your new labels as God's child: significant ... beautiful ... worthy ... ambassador ... princess ... mighty ... daughter ... saint ... apple of God's eye ... secure ... beloved.

Rahab escaped the walls of Jericho by identifying herself with the scarlet cord. You are redeemed from your old labels by identifying with the blood of Jesus Christ the moment you became a Christian.

Embrace Your New Identity

Rahab left the people, past, and culture that had confined her. She embraced her new identity as one of God's chosen people. If you are a Christian, you have been identified as a child of God by the blood of Jesus Christ. Perhaps it is time to leave the labels and the limitations behind so that you too can move into God's plan and purpose for your life.

Rahab had an extraordinary life. She passed down a legacy of faith and compassion to her children. Her son, Boaz, gave compassion and provision to a poor foreign widow named Ruth. I have no doubt Rahab's testimony played a huge role in Boaz's ability to see beyond Ruth's labels of "single," "outsider," and "lower-class." Boaz, the "guardian-redeemer" (Ruth 3:9), married Ruth and redeemed her from all her labels. The legacy of the "guardian-redeemer" continues through their family line right down to Jesus (Matthew 1:5–17).

Jesus, your guardian-redeemer, sees straight through those labels you wear. "Praise be to the LORD, who this day has not left you without a guardian-redeemer. May he become famous throughout Israel! He will renew your life and sustain you" (Ruth 4:14–15).

God renews your life by giving you a new identity as his child, making you an heir to his estate (Galatians 4:7). Not only do you have a new identity, but God also provides for your needs and makes the impossible, possible (Matthew 6: 25–34; Luke 1:37).

You serve a big God who has given you a dream in your heart to bring him glory. If you have received Christ, the glass slipper fits. Wear it and walk hand and hand with your Father to fulfill the calling on your life!

DAY 6

I am the vine; you are the branches. If you remain in me and I in you, you will bear much fruit; apart from me you can do nothing. —*John 15:5*

After Joshua rescued Rahab, she went to live with the Israelites. "Joshua spared Rahab the prostitute ... and she lives among the Israelites to this day" (Joshua 6:25). The word *lives* in that scripture is the Hebrew word *yashab*, which means to dwell, abide, or marry.[3] Not only did Rahab choose to abide with God's chosen people, but she also married an Israelite named Salmon. Rahab lived with the Israelites for the rest of her life, leaving behind the prostitution and paganism of her former life.

Complete Surrender

Our background might not include prostitution or worshiping golden idols, but if we are looking to someone or something else to find satisfaction or meet our needs, we are serving someone or something other than God. Anything we are holding on to tighter than we are holding on to God is an idol.

Can Christians have idols? Absolutely. What or whom are you depending on more than God to meet your needs?

When we completely surrender our lives, we see that God not only desires to fill us but also to satisfy our needs with the "finest of wheat; with honey from the rock" (see Psalm 81:8–16). The Rock is Jesus (1 Corinthians 10:4). Jesus also promises that we will never be thirsty when we drink his water (John 4:14). Jesus is the only one who can truly meet our every need. We will never be fulfilled until Christ becomes the center of our lives.

I believe most Christians truly want to put Christ on the throne of their hearts and leave idols behind, but we cannot do it on our own. However, if we are willing, *he* is able to do it through us.

Complete surrender is not about what you try to do, but with whom you are united. We do not have enough willpower to get rid of "self" and put Christ on the throne. However, the Holy Spirit can do it through us when we abide. Just as Rahab married into the Israelites and lived with them, Jesus Christ holds out his hand to his bride, the church, and says, "Come, abide with me."

Read John 15:1–17. What does it look like to abide? What happens when we choose daily to abide in Christ?

_____

_____

_____

Following in His Footsteps

Abiding, dwelling, and remaining with Jesus means staying close to him through a personal intimate relationship. We allow him to be a part of every area of our lives. We don't abide with him just while we pray or study our Bibles—we are aware of his presence throughout the day. Abiding is not trying to get more of God—it is all about allowing God to have more of us! Bearing fruit and yielding our will to his are natural extensions of an intimate fellowship with Christ.

Living completely for God includes keeping Jesus' commands. Keeping his commands is not following a list of religious rules—it is following in his footsteps. We listen to his voice and yield our will to his. We can hear and follow his voice when we stay close to the vine. Trying to keep the law through our own strength, and following the Holy Spirit's lead in our lives through abiding in Christ is the difference between religion and relationship.

During one season of my life, God called me away from all ministry, telling me to simply listen and follow him. My eyes were opened to what it meant to be led by the Spirit. Loving others, joy, and bearing fruit occurred as I got out of the way and allowed Christ to live through me.

That season of following in Jesus' footsteps ended when gaining the approval of others captivated my attention again. God never left my side. I was simply choosing to listen to another voice.

The gospel set me free to return to the voice of truth. The only barriers to an intimate relationship with God are ones we create. God's arms are always open to us. The gospel was preached so that you could choose to live for God! (1 Peter 4:6)

It Is Our Choice

God will never force us to have an intimate relationship with him because he gives us free will. After we become Christians, we are free to surrender to him day by day, moment by moment. God's perfect plan allows us to choose so that our relationship is based on love, not duty. Love is a choice. Relationship is a choice. I have heard it said, you do what you love with passion. You do what you have to do with obligation.

The more I experience an intimate relationship with Jesus, the more I want to stay there. Jesus has opened the door through his grace for an intimate relationship. He never leaves our side. It is our choice moment by moment to abide with him. The choice becomes clearer and clearer as God prunes us.

Expect to Be Pruned

When we abide with Jesus, we *will* experience pruning seasons (John 15:2). You cannot fully surrender in your own might. God is the gardener who prunes away all those branches that are not bearing fruit. God will prune out of your life all those areas you want to surrender, but can't. "Since Jesus went through everything you're going through and more, learn to think like him. Think of your sufferings as a weaning from that old sinful habit of always expecting to get your own way. Then you'll be able to live out your days free to pursue what God wants instead of being tyrannized by what you want." (1 Peter 4:1–2 MSG)

Dealing with difficulties offers an opportunity to grow. Trust God in your brokenness. He is not the author of your pain, but God will use it all to build you into a mighty warrior of God. "Consider it pure joy, my brothers and sisters, whenever you face trials of many kinds, because you know that the testing of your faith produces perseverance. Let perseverance finish its work so that you may be mature and complete, not lacking anything" (James 1:2–4).

At one time my son went through a very difficult period. As I look back, I can see how God was pruning fear out of our family. The pruning was painful. We were broken, but when we came through, our faith flourished. As painful as it was, I would not trade that season of my life for anything. My son learned a new dependence on God that I never could have taught him. I received a deeper understanding of God's grace. Our prayer life as a family increased and we all saw God move mountains.

This growth in our family did not happen from trying harder to be good. The Lord did some of his gardening through brokenness.

When you become a Christian, you become a new creation. When you choose to abide, God works through his Word, your circumstances, and the power of the Holy Spirit to prune away all those barren branches that do not belong in the new you.

God's Word Is Our Map

Part of abiding involves allowing the Word to remain in us (John 15:3, 7). There is a powerful relationship between the Word and the Holy Spirit. Joshua needed both in the Promised Land (Deuteronomy 34:9; Joshua 1:9). The Word is our map and the Holy Spirit is our guide. Jesus said the Word cleanses us, sanctifies us, and provides us daily bread, essential for our daily living (John 15:3, 17:17; Matthew 4:4).

God's Word Builds Faith

Jesus said, "If you remain in me and my words remain in you, ask whatever you wish, and it will be done for you" (John 15:7). The Word enables us to pray with confidence for God's will for our lives.

God delights in answering his children's prayers (Luke 7:9–15). We can ask for anything that is in line with the Father's will, and we can understand God's will for our lives through the Word of God. The Word sanctifies our prayers to line up with God's will for our lives.

When you abide, God will ask you to do things beyond your abilities. Come boldly before the throne. The mountain mover is on your side! Praying Scripture is powerful and effective because it opens our eyes to God's power available for every believer (Ephesians 1:17–19).

All this said, I am not suggesting that God gives us whatever we want when we want it. You cannot manipulate God. All prayers are submitted above all to God's will—his plan and timing (see Luke 22:39–46). We can pray with confidence and then rest in the absolute assurance that God loves us.

Jesus Gives Us Joy—in Every Circumstance

You know what else happens when we choose to abide? The Bible says that our joy is complete (John 15:11). Perhaps when God revealed something that you needed to leave behind, you thought you would be missing all the fun. WRONG. Jesus came to give you joy!

Christians should be the most joyful people in the world. Following a list of rules does not give us joy. Legalism will kill our joy. The ministry of the Spirit gives life! You may be religious and never experience joy, but building a relationship with Jesus and abiding in him brings abundant and constant joy.

"God is love. Whoever lives in love lives in God, and God in him" (1 John 4:16). Through abiding, we allow God to love through us. We are filled with his love and it spills out to those around us. As Christians, we are called to love even our enemies. This kind of love is supernatural and only comes through an intimate relationship with God.

Rahab followed the Israelites and decided she could not live without them. Choosing to live with the Israelites for the rest of her life, Rahab left prostitution and paganism and lived happily ever after.

Your happily-ever-after stands at the door and knocks. Jesus does not promise a life with no pain or problems. But he promises that as we abide in him, he will be with us—and he will make it possible for us to experience joy in every circumstance.

The choice is not to *do* but to *yield*. It is a dance, if you will, and we are keeping in step with the Spirit (Galatians 5:25). It is a moment-by-moment decision to follow the person of the Holy Spirit, because apart from Jesus you can do nothing (John 15:5). You are God's child; Jesus Christ holds out his hand wanting to satisfy you with the finest wheat and honey from the rock. What are you waiting for?

Chapter 4
THE NEW COVENANT

My nourish notes for Joshua 3:1–5:12

Day 1: Reveal

Meditate on the scriptures, prayerfully reading and reflecting on the verses. Mark the phrases, verses, or words that catch your attention. Journal and learn more as the Lord leads you.

Day 2: Respond

Respond to activate truth in your life. The **IMPACT** acronym provides questions to help you apply the Word. Sometimes you may not have an answer to all six questions.

Image of God to trust? *An attribute of God, Jesus, or the Holy Spirit to trust.*

Message to share? *A word of encouragement, truth, or a prayer to share with others.*

Promise to treasure? *A promise in the Bible to stand on by faith.*

Action to take? *A specific step God is calling you to take.*

Core authentic identity to embrace? *A truth about how God sees you to agree with in your heart.*

Transgression to confess or forgive? *A confession to receive healing, help, and restoration through Christ.*

Day 3: Renew

Carry God's Word with you during the week. Renew your mind daily by focusing on one word, verse, or truth that the Holy Spirit revealed through the Bible. Like an anchor that secures its vessel, renewing your mind with the truth brings security and focus, despite the waves you face during the day.

My Anchor of Truth:

NOURISH JOURNAL

Additional space to record any further thoughts God has shared with me.

DAY 4

I pray that the eyes of your heart may be enlightened in order that you may know the hope to which he has called you, the riches of his glorious inheritance in his holy people, and his incomparably great power for us who believe. That power is the same as the mighty strength he exerted when he raised Christ from the dead and seated him at his right hand in the heavenly realms. —*Ephesians 1:18–20*

"There has got to be something more in my walk with God," I confessed to a friend as our children played on the playground.

At the time, I was in a Bible study that focused on Acts and the Epistles. In Ephesians, Paul prayed that believers would know the riches of their glorious inheritance and the resurrection power within them (Ephesians 1:19). Where was that in my life?

I had been a Christian for eight years, read my Bible, prayed, and attended church … but I felt there had to be more. In Acts, I saw the early Christians, in every sense ambassadors of Christ, drawing on all that Christ had died to give them. I examined my own Christianity. It was full of ministry, Bible study, and church attendance. I was busy but not fruitful.

Jesus came to fill us with streams of living water, but on the inside, I felt a spiritual dryness. With tears in my eyes, I told my friend, "I am so weary of reading about a deeper life in Christ. I want to experience it, but I don't know how."

Discovering Our New Covenant Position in Christ

That day was the beginning of a new journey that would take me on a deeper walk with God. I am still on that journey today.

My friend and her father prayed with me. I began to learn many things about the blessings of the new covenant, a life transformed from the inside. The truth of the gospel set me free to leave the dry desert and cross over the Jordan to enjoy the fruit of my new covenant position in Christ.

For every New Testament principle, there is an Old Testament picture. I believe chapters 3 through 5 of Joshua illustrate the new covenant. We can partake of our spiritual inheritance because of our new covenant position.

The Lord commanded the Israelites three times to keep the ark of the covenant ahead of them while they crossed over the Jordan River (Joshua 3:3, 6, 11). Keep your new covenant position always before you. The more you understand the new covenant, the more truth you will know about your spiritual inheritance … and the more you will see that there is an open door to go deeper with God and walk in the freedom that Christ purchased with his blood.

Don't Stay in the Wilderness

Even though God had opened the door for me to walk more intimately with him, for a long time I had been unaware of all that my spiritual inheritance had to offer. I had sat in the wilderness and never crossed over into the Promised Land.

The Israelites were freed from slavery in Egypt but wandered in the wilderness for forty years before they possessed their spiritual inheritance. I was freed from the penalty of sin by becoming a Christian, yet I was wandering around in the wilderness of the old covenant of the law instead of entering the new covenant of the Spirit (2 Corinthians 3:6).

Jesus Christ paid the price for our sin with his life so that you and I could come under the new covenant and experience all the love, blessings, transformation, protection, and power over sin that an intimate relationship with God has to offer.

Love is a choice … God will never force you to take advantage of your inheritance. Jesus died for much more than just to provide us with a "pass" into heaven. God has a covenant with his children, allowing them to receive a divine inheritance (Galatians 4:5–7).

Perhaps you are in the wilderness looking longingly over into the land filled with milk and honey. You attend church, read your Bible, and pray, but you know there has to be something more. Your Lord and Savior is pursuing you. Turn around. He wanted you so much that he sent his Son to die so that the blessings of a new covenant life, a life transformed from the inside, could be yours.

God Works Through Covenants

Unlike today's contracts, which are sometimes easily broken, covenants in biblical times were binding. The Hebrew word for covenant is *berith*, which means to *cut until blood flows*. When a covenant was made, an animal was sacrificed and the two parties walked between the streams of flowing blood.[1] First John 5:6 says, "This is the one who came by water and blood—Jesus Christ. He did not come by water only, but by water and blood." When Jesus was sacrificed on the cross, a Roman soldier pierced his side and a sudden flow of blood AND water came out of his body (John 19:34). The Israelites walked between the waters in the Jordan River to reach their inheritance. We walk through the blood of Jesus as we covenant with God, confessing with our mouths and believing in our hearts that Jesus is Lord over our lives (Romans 10:10).

God works through covenants to establish relationships with his people. The old covenant was made on Mount Sinai in the wilderness and involved man trying to save himself by keeping the law. The old covenant reveals to people their need for the new covenant because no man can keep the law. All have sinned. The law cannot save anyone. The new covenant is all about God making a covenant with himself by sacrificing his Son, Jesus

Christ. Jesus, the only one to live without sin, fulfilled the old covenant and provided a new way.

Jesus Is the Mediator

God asked the priests to stand in the middle of the Jordan River. God asked his only Son to stand in the gap for you and me, becoming the mediator of the new covenant. Jesus—the Great High Priest, the King of Glory—always intercedes for every believer. The reason we can count on all the promises our new covenant relationship brings, is that Jesus, who was without sin, keeps it for us! Hebrews 9:15 says, "Christ is the mediator of a new covenant, that those who are called may receive the promised eternal inheritance—now that he has died as a ransom to set them free from the sins committed under the first covenant." God made the covenant with himself, and Jesus Christ is the mediator (Hebrews 6:13–20, 7:23–9:15).

I don't know about you, but if I were going to cross a mile-wide river at flood stage, I would want to be certain that the waters would be cut off until I reached the other side.[2] The priests, standing in the middle of the riverbed, were Israel's assurance that God would be faithful to hold the waters back until the nation of Israel crossed over.

Jesus is your assurance that all the promises of God are yes and amen (2 Corinthians 1:20). There is not an addiction he cannot overcome, a stronghold he cannot break, a sin he cannot forgive, a burden he cannot bear, a broken heart he cannot restore, a sickness he cannot heal. He lives to intercede for you.

If the ark and the priest were valuable to God, how much more so was his Son? Looking at the river in the natural realm, the Israelites would have seen that it was impossible for the entire nation to cross the Jordan. But they chose to see the situation in the spiritual realm, keeping their eyes focused on the priests and the ark, and they were assured of God's faithfulness.

What promises from God seem impossible to you? Could it perhaps be that you have your eyes on the river and not the Redeemer?

Covenants Bring Intertwining Lives

The Greek word in the New Testament for covenant is *diatheke*, which means *the disposition of property, as in the last will and testament*. A covenant in biblical times was a sacred exchange of property between two parties. Garments, weapons, lands, promises, and blessings were traded. After covenants were made, names were changed. For example, Abram became Abraham.[3]

When I married my husband, I entered into a covenant relationship with him. My last name was changed from Greene to Thompson, symbolic of the fact that we now belonged to each other. Our lives became intertwined.

The participants of a covenant agreed to honor the covenant even if that meant death. Lives were laid down for each other, and promises of protection and provision were made. Jonathan and David made a covenant to protect each other (1 Samuel 20:16–17).[4] Family members and their descendants were also included in the covenant. Because of their covenant of friendship, David sought out Jonathan's son Mephibosheth after Jonathan's death. Mephibosheth was poor and crippled. David brought him into his house, promised to restore his land, gave him provision, and allowed him to eat at the king's table forever (2 Samuel 9:1–9).

And so, as we enter into the new covenant, our lives are intertwined with Jesus.

Experience the Whole Banquet

As a child, I lived on a diet of peanut butter and honey sandwiches. When I was five years old, we went to my grandmother's house for Thanksgiving dinner—a real family event. Every piece of silver was polished and placed on the table with beautiful pressed napkins, flowers, and lit candles. A sumptuous turkey and roasted lamb crowned the table. Corn and oyster casserole, fresh green beans, stuffing, and sweet potatoes were just a few of the dishes. Dessert time brought homemade cakes and pies. It was truly a table fit for a king.

After the blessing, my grandmother came and wrapped her arms around me, saying, "Now Aliene, what can I get you to eat?" I looked at all that was spread out before me and said, "I'll take a peanut butter and honey sandwich." My grandmother was surprised but went into the kitchen and returned with my request.

As Christians under the new covenant, King Jesus has spread out a banquet for us. We have to let go and look beyond our peanut butter to experience it. Just as I never thought to venture beyond peanut butter and honey sandwiches, we can so easily fall into the routine of religion and never venture deeper with God. Why would you ever settle for peanut butter sandwiches when you, like Mephibosheth, can dine with the King?

When we dine with Jesus, we participate in all that our new covenant relationship has to offer. There is a divine exchange between Christ and us. Hudson Taylor, the great missionary, refers to this as "the exchanged life."[5] Christ lives in us. All that he has is ours. I, like Mephibosheth, am poor in many ways (poor in righteousness, love, strength, power), and yet Jesus, the King, is rich in all those things and more (Galatians 5).[6]

What does that mean? Read the next paragraph aloud.

Jesus took all my sin and gave me a right standing with God. Jesus took all my sorrows and gave me his joy. He took all my anxiety and gave me his peace. Jesus took all of my shame and allowed me to hold my head up high. He took all my weakness and gave me his mighty strength through the power of his Spirit. He gave me the armor of God for my protection against the enemy's attacks (Ephesians 6:10–19). He took all of my sickness and depression and healed me body, soul, and spirit (Matthew 8:17; Isaiah 53). He crucified my flesh and gave me the fruit of the Spirit (Galatians 5). Everything that Jesus had, all that his name means, all that his life represents, is mine. He lives on the inside of me. God has given me access to eat from his table and share in the inheritance because of Jesus Christ. Spiritually, he broke the power of sin in my life. He took my religion and gave me a relationship. He took my fear and gave me love (1 John 4:18). He bound up my broken heart (Isaiah 61:1) and proclaimed my freedom. Jesus took my filthy rags and adorned me with a robe of righteousness and a garment of praise (Isaiah 61:3). The curse of the law is broken (Galatians 3:13). And now I am free to have the power of his Spirit (Acts 1:8) and choose to walk into a new way of life.

Our new covenant position promises the power and presence of God's Spirit to equip us for service and to transform us to be more like Christ (Ezekiel 36:26).

A Life Transformed Within

In the garden of Eden, God began dwelling with man. After the fall, man built altars. Then God instructed Moses to build the tabernacle, complete with the ark of the covenant, where he dwelt (2 Samuel 6:2). Next, Solomon built a stationary temple in Jerusalem. One day, Emmanuel, God with Us—Jesus Christ—came to dwell among us. After his death and resurrection, our bodies became the temple and his Spirit dwelt within us. Finally, in the New Jerusalem the dwelling of God will be with men, and he will live with them (Revelation 21:3).

Today, our bodies are the temple, and the Holy Spirit dwells inside of every believer. Jesus breathed on the disciples and said, "Receive the Holy Spirit" (John 20:22). If you are a Christian, you have received the Holy Spirit. Did you hear me? The Spirit of the living God lives on the inside of you! However, it is one thing to have something and quite another to *use* it.

We have a heating system installed in our home, but in order for heat to fill my house the thermostat has to be turned on. The phrase "filled with the Spirit" has blessed many and yet caused division within the church. The Holy Spirit moves God's children in different ways, and I do not believe it is right to demand that our way is "right," any more than the Jewish believers demanding circumcision for the Gentiles was right (Acts 10). Nor should the controversy keep us quiet about the Holy Spirit. In the book of Acts, the phrase "filled with the Spirit" is used repeatedly in conjunction with believers doing amazing acts of service for God's glory (Acts 4:8, 31; 6:3, 5; 7:55; 9:17; 13:9; 13:52).

If we are honest with ourselves we will eventually come to a place where we realize that we cannot serve God in our own strength. When we come to the end of ourselves, we can finally raise our hands in surrender and say, "Lord, I cannot do what you are asking me to do on my own strength. I am no longer going to try all this on my own. Empty me of myself and fill me with your Holy Spirit that I may be a vessel to bring you glory." "He must become greater; I must become less" (John 3:30).

I believe a transformed life is the most amazing miracle God performs. Before the Israelites crossed the Jordan, Joshua told them to consecrate themselves because God was going to do amazing things among them. *Consecration* means *to be set apart for the Lord*. Your heart for his glory. God fills us with the Holy Spirit to make us holy, equip us for service, and help us point others to Christ as we yield to him. The Person of the Holy Spirit thrives in a vessel emptied of self. Then we become more sensitive to God's promptings, and the Holy Spirit can work through us to accomplish God's will.

Sanctification is the work of the Spirit. He will purify our hearts so that the gifts of the Spirit operating through us, and a life spent sharing his love, will *bring glory to him*. Nothing brings more glory to God than the testimony of a transformed life. We cannot become holy on our own effort; we need the fullness of the Holy Spirit, yielding to his lead in our lives.

Entering the Promised Land

The Israelites passed through "God-parted" waters twice. Crossing the Red Sea, they left a life of slavery. Crossing the Jordan, they left the wilderness and entered into the Promised Land.

When Jesus immerses us in the Holy Spirit, we step into the living waters and are filled with God's love and power that overflow as we reach out to others. We are filled to be fruitful, holy, and to bring glory to God.

Before the Israelites fought their battles in the Promised Land, they crossed through the Jordan River. Before Jesus began his ministry on earth, he was baptized in the Jordan River, and the Holy Spirit descended upon him. Before the disciples began the Great Commission, Jesus told them, "Wait for the gift my Father promised, which you have heard me speak about. For John baptized with water, but in a few days you will be baptized with the Holy Spirit" (Acts 1:4–5, 8).

There is not enough determination and willpower inside of you to overcome your sin and fulfill your calling without the Holy Spirit. All of us who want to make an impact for the kingdom of God need the power of the Holy Spirit. Ken Abraham in his book *Positive Holiness* writes,

> If you study Church history carefully, you will quickly discover that great Christians throughout the years have described some experience subsequent to their salvation whereby they entered into a deeper relationship with Christ. The terms they used to describe this experience vary widely, but if you distill and discern the common denominators of their experience, you will discover that they were talking about a life of holiness, a life that is surrendered to and controlled by the Holy Spirit.

Nor are their testimonies restricted to individuals of similar theological persuasions, nationalities, race, sex, or life-style. Men and women as disparate as Hudson Taylor, A.B. Simpson, Andrew Murray, Dwight L. Moody, Harold John Ockenga, Phoebe Palmer, Oswald Chambers, Amy Carmichael, Blaise Pascal, Charles Finney, Corrie ten Boom, A. J. Gordon, John Bunyan, Ian Thomas, and a host of others all bear witness to an experience that took place at some point after their salvation, an experience that totally revolutionized their Christian lives as much or in some cases more so than their conversion had transformed them."[7]

The Spirit brings life. There was nothing wrong with the manna the Israelites ate in the wilderness, but it was no substitute for the fruit in the Promised Land. The ministry of the law "came with glory," but it is no substitute for the ministry of the Spirit, which is even "more glorious" (2 Corinthians 3:9–11).

Do you feel as if you are in a spiritual wilderness? What is God asking you to do that is beyond your own strength? Whom is God asking you to love that you cannot love on your own? What sin pattern do you feel is impossible to break? More love (Romans 5:5), more power (Ephesians 1:18–20), and more freedom (2 Corinthians 3:17) are on the King's table. He loves you and has prepared a place for you to dine at his table. *Brave heart*, Christianity that requires courage, rather than Christianity that demands comfort, requires you to stand in the New Covenant strength that only God can provide.

The Roads Will Not Always Be Smooth

Becoming a *brave heart* will take you on new roads. God told the Israelites that he was going to take them to places they had never seen before (Joshua 3:4). What new roads is the Great Shepherd asking you to travel? Joshua followed him through flooding waters, into battles fought with trumpets (Joshua 6), and into lands unknown.

Becoming a *brave heart* will take you on rough roads. Living under the new covenant does not mean we will have an easy life. In fact, God promised just the opposite. Jesus said, "In this world you will have trouble. But take heart! I have overcome the world" (John 16:33).

Are You Ready?

New Roads. Rough Roads. God is counting on you and me to receive all that is given to us through the new covenant so that we can do his work on earth. You may have rivers at flood stage raging all around you in the natural, but Jesus Christ is standing in the gap of the Jordan waiting for you to cross over into a deeper life with him. The striving is over. Your position has been secured through the blood of Christ. It is your responsibility and your great privilege to believe it and walk as an ambassador on earth for Christ—not by *your* might but by *his* Spirit.

DAY 5

He has made us competent as ministers of a new covenant—
not of the letter but of the Spirit; for the letter kills, but the Spirit gives life.
—2 Corinthians 3:6

God has called all believers to be ministers of the new covenant. He has richly blessed you in every way through the new covenant so that you can pour out those blessings to the world. At this point, you might be tempted to look inward and focus only on getting your own needs met. However, the blessings we receive from the new covenant are provision for us to give to others. When we let our lights shine, we build memorials to point others to Christ. That is the new-covenant ministry. God told Joshua, "Today I will begin to exalt you in the eyes of all Israel, so they may know that I am with you" (Joshua 3:7). God gives us the new covenant so that we will exalt the name of Jesus. He gives us the fruit of the Spirit (Galatians 5) and the gifts of the Spirit (1 Corinthians 12)—not to bring glory to ourselves, but to bring glory to Jesus Christ.

Reaching Out to Others

God called Nancy Alcorn to step out in faith and start a home for hurting young women. Over the years, countless women have come to stay at Mercy Ministries. Some who come do not know Jesus; others have been in church all their lives. All the young women are immersed in unconditional love, bathed in the Word of God, and taught who they are in Christ. Unwed mothers with no place to turn find peace and provision at the doors of Mercy. Girls captured in the prison of alcoholism and drugs find freedom from their addictions. Young ladies arrive at Mercy's doors suffering from eating disorders, depression, or self-harm and leave healed by Jesus and equipped by the Holy Spirit to make a difference in this world.

I first heard about Mercy Ministries when Nancy Alcorn was featured on TV. Testimonies from two young women delivered from depression, drug addiction, and eating disorders touched my heart. Since that day, my husband and I have supported Mercy. At the time, I had no idea how God would use Mercy to change me.

I loved the ministry so much that one summer I visited a Mercy home in Nashville. A resident in the program began to share how Mercy had changed her life. She said to me, "Aliene, you don't understand. I have been to six different hospitals, and no one could fix me but this place." I realized in that moment that I was looking at a miracle. I knew beyond any doubt that all of God's promises are true. The same God who made a covenant with that young lady made a covenant with me. Christ is still the Healer. The power of sin has been broken. There is no addiction, no lifestyle, and no destructive emotion he cannot help us overcome.

Nancy's life's work is a memorial to the power of the cross and the promises of the new covenant. I have never met a woman who followed God so intently. No matter how impossible things looked, Nancy took the Mountain Mover at his Word. Nancy Alcorn is my modern-day Joshua. She is my hero. It was never God's will for young women to be captive to those prisons. Jesus called Nancy Alcorn to start Mercy Ministries so that countless young women could find freedom from their pain and suffering in the unconditionally loving arms of Jesus. That is new-covenant ministry: making memorials to the power of the cross with our lives in order to point others to Jesus.

Building Memorials

In biblical times, after covenants were established, memorials were made to remind future generations of the covenant.[8] After the Israelites crossed over the Jordan, God instructed Joshua to make a memorial out of stones. Joshua appointed twelve men, one from each tribe, to retrieve a stone from the middle of the Jordan where the priests held the ark of the covenant. Each man took up a stone and carried it on his shoulder to Gilgal, where Joshua set up the stones. The memorial was built to remind the Israelites of God's mighty power and so that they might always follow him (Joshua 4:24).

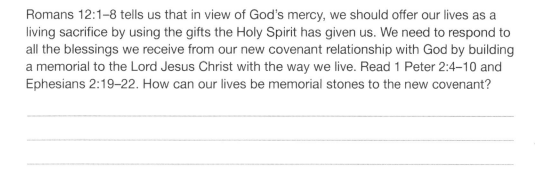

> Romans 12:1–8 tells us that in view of God's mercy, we should offer our lives as a living sacrifice by using the gifts the Holy Spirit has given us. We need to respond to all the blessings we receive from our new covenant relationship with God by building a memorial to the Lord Jesus Christ with the way we live. Read 1 Peter 2:4–10 and Ephesians 2:19–22. How can our lives be memorial stones to the new covenant?

This is new-covenant ministry. We are blessed so that we can bring blessings to others. God loves you unconditionally so you can love others unconditionally. God gives to you so you can give to others. God fills you with the Holy Spirit so you can bring others a drink of living water. Christ has reconciled you to God, and now you have a ministry of reconciliation. God comforts you so you can comfort others. God has forgiven you, so you can give grace and mercy to others. God has lifted you out of your pit so you can lift others out of their pits. God has called us to set up memorials to serve as signs to future generations that Christ is still the answer. There is a hurting world out there that is looking for unconditional love and help that they can find only in Jesus.

A Team Effort

Joshua told twelve men to carry one stone each to contribute to the memorial. If one tribe member had tried to carry all twelve stones, the burden would have been heavy and the load too much to bear. If one tribe member had become jealous of another person's stone, there could have been strife. If one tribe member had decided to just sit and watch the other tribe members carry their stones, instead of obeying God by doing his part, the memorial would not be complete. Thankfully, each tribe member carried his own stone, and the memorial was built with each one doing his own part.

God calls all of us to be ministers of the new covenant, but he gives us all different stones to carry by giving us different gifts, passions, and dreams. You are a designer's original! Do not make the mistake of competing and comparing yourself with other women. Competition in God's kingdom is unnecessary. Just like our gifts and callings, each stone has its place and is a vital part of the memorial (Romans 12:4–5). Be true to yourself. Christians who make a difference focus on their own calling (John 21:17–25; Colossians 4:17).

Jesus, the Cornerstone

Jesus is the chief cornerstone. Bring your gifts to him, and in his divine plan, he will put them together for his glory. All the men brought their stones to Joshua, and he put them together to build the memorial. We never really know how God is going to use our gifts. God has the big picture. Be faithful to give your all to God and allow him to do the rest.

Jesus said to his disciples, "Whoever wants to be my disciple must deny themselves and take up their cross daily and follow me" (Luke 9:23). Our death to self births the glorification of Christ.

One day a man named Simon of Cyrene carried the cross for the Lord Jesus Christ across his shoulders. Joshua asked the Israelites to carry their stones on their shoulders. Jesus Christ asks you to carry your cross.

Every day we can carry the cross for Jesus to the world by bringing his kingdom on earth as it is in heaven. You are Christ's ambassador, and when others see fruit in you, you are a living stone built on the foundation of the cornerstone of Christ. Every time you bless others instead of curse them, you have laid a memory stone to God's glory. Every time you choose to forgive or encourage someone, you have laid a memory stone. When sorrow fills your soul and you choose joy, when worry and doubt engulf you and you choose to trust God … you have laid another stone in the kingdom. When you choose to praise instead of complain … every time you follow Spirit over the flesh … you have carried the cross of Jesus here on earth.

God's kingdom will be built on earth through you and me when we lay down our fears and selfish desires and live for him. You do not necessarily have to be a part of some big ministry to bring his kingdom here on earth—it can happen through your moment-by-moment lifestyle choices. Right in your backyard, in your workplace, at your children's school, you can be a living memorial for the Lord Jesus Christ. Jesus said, "Let your light shine before others, that they may see your good deeds and glorify your Father in heaven" (Matthew 5:16). If you want to get others interested in Jesus, let your light shine.

What Kind of Memorial Are You Building?

God offers the gifts of the Spirit and fruit of the Spirit to bring glory to God. Joshua 4:9 says that the stones laid for the memorial "are there to this day." Who are some Christians you know whose lives are still making an impact because of the new-covenant memorials they built?

Mercy Ministries is an example of a living stone memorial that continues to bring glory to Jesus Christ. Every changed life from Mercy is another stone. Those girls leave Mercy and plant themselves all over the world, declaring God's praise as they in turn reach out to others to share the gospel. Mercy Ministries is a memorial stone that is still here to this day and I believe will continue to impact future generations.

What do you want to change? Surrendered to the Holy Spirit, you have his influence to leave a legacy. Will you lay down your life to make a memorial to the Lord Jesus Christ? What stone has he asked you to pick up? Where has he asked you to build a memorial? Hey, *brave heart*! Yeah, that's you. Let's use all that God has given us to leave a legacy that honors him.

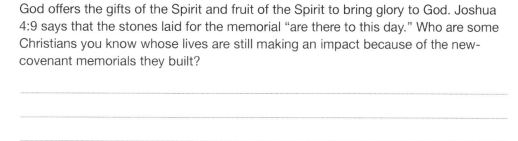

Key Treasure

What do you want to change? Surrendered to the Holy Spirit, you have his influence to leave a legacy.

DAY 6

What shall we say, then? Shall we go on sinning so that grace may increase? By no means! We are those who have died to sin; how can we live in it any longer? Or don't you know that all of us who were baptized into Christ Jesus were baptized into his death? We were therefore buried with him through baptism into death in order that, just as Christ was raised from the dead through the glory of the Father, we too may live a new life.

For if we have been united with him in a death like his, we will certainly also be united with him in a resurrection like his. For we know that our old self was crucified with him so that the body ruled by sin might be done away with, that we should no longer be slaves to sin—because anyone who has died has been set free from sin."
—Romans 6:1–7

The kings of the Amorites and the kings of the Canaanites were shaking in their boots. Just like Rahab, they heard that Israel's God had parted the Jordan and was headed their way. Safely on the other side of the Jordan, the Israelites set up a base camp at Gilgal. Before the Israelites moved out from their camp to capture Jericho, they had to take care of some family business to prepare them for battle. Circumcision reestablished their identity with the covenant God had made with Abraham. Eating the Passover meal, the Israelites celebrated God's mighty power to deliver them. God wanted them to remember in the days to come, in the heat of the battle when those spears from the enemy were coming, that they could count on him.

Circumcision of the Heart

Covenants in biblical times were sealed by a permanent physical mark made on the body as a sign of the covenant. Meals were also shared to commemorate the covenant. The mark and the meal helped both parties to remember the agreements made to each other.[9]

The covenant God made with Abraham was the birth of the new covenant that all Christians are a part of today (Galatians 3:13–14, 4:28–29). God said to Abraham, "You are to undergo circumcision, and it will be the sign of the covenant between me and you" (Genesis 17:11). Every male and all foreigners living among the Israelites were to be circumcised in Abraham's household and in generations to come. The covenant promised that the land of Canaan belonged to the Israelites. Circumcision was a sign that pointed to the promise. The Israelites could fight Jericho with confidence because God had promised that the land was theirs.

When you became a Christian, Jesus circumcised your heart by the Holy Spirit and made you dead to sin but alive to Christ (Romans 2:29). Colossians 2:11–12 says, "In him you were also circumcised with a circumcision not performed by human hands. Your whole self ruled by the flesh was put off when you were circumcised by Christ, having been buried with him in baptism, in which you were also raised with him through your faith in the working of God, who raised him from the dead." Baptism is the public outward sign of what Christ did inwardly the moment you became a Christian. Just as circumcision did not make Abraham righteous (Romans 4:11), baptism does not make you a Christian. In baptism, we identify with Christ's death, burial, and resurrection. We are saying publicly, "My identity is now in Christ. My old self was crucified and he lives in me. Through my faith and reliance on the power of God, I can now live for God."

> God promised the Israelites the land of Canaan. According to Romans 6:1–14, what has God promised you?

When you became a Christian, sin lost its control over your life. The power of sin has been broken and you can live for God. Circumcision involves cutting off something that is no longer needed. Christ circumcises your old self because it is no longer needed. You are no longer helpless against sin. Now freed from the law and your old self, you can, through the power of the Holy Spirit, choose to live for God.

Our Identity Is in Christ

In the past those scriptures in Romans did not make me feel like celebrating. Instead, I felt very condemned and frustrated because, although was I born again, I still struggled with sin. Instead of allowing these scriptures to empower me, I felt defeated. I was focused on myself and my failures—naturally, I felt defeated! However, my identity is in Christ. When I focus on his goodness, the truth of my baptism becomes a reality because I am depending on Christ's victory over sin, not my own.

Jesus disarmed Satan at the cross and will not allow him to take away your new-covenant identity. Satan has no real authority, but he can deceive you into believing that you have no power over sin. Neil Anderson, in his book *The Bondage Breaker* writes,

> Nothing is more foundational to your freedom from Satan's bondage than understanding and affirming what God has done for you in Christ and who you are as His child. Your attitudes, actions, responses and reactions to life's circumstances are greatly affected by what you believe about yourself. If you see yourself as the helpless victim of Satan and his schemes, you will probably live like a victim and be in bondage to his lies. But if you see yourself as a dearly loved and accepted child of God, you will have a better chance of living like one.[10]

The Israelites chose to fight their battles in the Promised Land because of a promise God made to Abraham years before. Although it did not happen overnight, the Lord fought for Israel. Because they chose to walk by faith, seven years later the land was theirs.

God has promised us that the power of sin is broken. You no longer *have* to yield to sin; you are free to live for God. You may still "feel" like you are not a conqueror, but God wants you to walk by faith and not by sight. The enemy will keep trying to remind you that you are still bound to your temptations, your issues, your childhood past, and your flesh. Why? If Satan can get you to believe the lies, you will act according to what you believe.

Even if we miss the mark and sin, when we are identified with Christ, Satan can no longer accuse us because the reproach has been rolled away. The Lord told Joshua, "'Today I have rolled away the reproach of Egypt from you.' So the place has been called Gilgal to this day" (Joshua 5:9). Egypt symbolizes slavery to sin and shame. The word *reproach* means in Hebrew *a taunt, a scorn, resting upon condition of shame, disgrace.*[11] The Bible says that Satan accuses and taunts Christians day and night and fills them with shame (Revelation 12:10).

Condemnation is never from God. Christ rolled away our shame through his sacrifice. If you feel like a bad Christian, Satan is trying to make you feel defeated by accusing you. Open your mouth and say, "Jesus rolled away my reproach, and your tactic to make me feel unworthy to be a Christian does not work anymore."

It Is a Process

Gilgal means a wheel or rolling.[12] Joshua and the Israelites will retreat to Gilgal again and again. We must continue to meditate on the truth of who we are in Christ to renew our minds and to be transformed. We do not learn it once and rest. Remember your baptism and all that it symbolizes. We remind ourselves repeatedly so that when the attacks come, we can stand in the truth.

Communion is a wonderful way to remember our new-covenant position. Before the battle of Jericho, the Israelites celebrated the Passover meal and remembered God's faithfulness (Exodus 12:14–16; Deuteronomy 16:1–8). On the eve of Jesus' crucifixion, the disciples celebrated the Passover with each other. The events that followed would test their faith. Jesus wanted them to remember that he was the Passover lamb and that his death would bring victory.

> And he took bread, gave thanks and broke it, and gave it to them, saying, "This is my body given for you; do this in remembrance of me." In the same way, after the supper he took the cup, saying, "This cup is the new covenant in my blood, which is poured out for you" (Luke 22:19–20).

Just as God cut the waters of the Jordan River to assure the Israelites that he would drive out their enemies, he cut covenant on the cross to disarm Satan to assure us that we will win with God. When the Israelites were standing in the Jordan, Joshua told them that they would know that the living God was among them and would drive out the Canaanites, the Hittites, the Hivites, the Perizzites, the Girgashites, the Amorites, and the Jebusites. God was assuring them that he would take care of all of their enemies.

Satan will still growl at you, tempt you, accuse you day and night, and try to wreak havoc in your life. He is still the prince of this world. Even Jesus was not free from being tempted by Satan, but he never yielded to those temptations (Matthew 4:1–11).

Jesus is greater than the prince of this world. Christ has secured your position. Now it is your responsibility to believe him. Christ has given you the armor of God. It is your responsibility to fight the enemy God's way. Through Jesus, we already have the victory (1 John 4:4). It is a done deal. You can count on it because of the new covenant.

When we celebrate Communion, we celebrate the provision for us in the blood of the Lamb and the broken body of Christ. By partaking of the bread, we celebrate the divine exchange and Christ as our hope of glory. By partaking of the wine, we celebrate the blood of Jesus Christ that continually cleanses us of our sins. *Thank you, Jesus, that you have freed me from the bondage of sin. You have redeemed me with your outstretched arms and delivered me from death. By your stripes, I have been healed. By your blood, I am forgiven* (Isaiah 53:5).

Jesus commanded us to celebrate Communion often. We must not forget the importance of taking Communion. Communion reminds us that Christ's death is our gain and encourages us to live the life Christ died to give us.

Celebrate Communion with other believers, around the dinner table with your family, and in those quiet moments when you are alone with Jesus. Every time you do, take time to remember your new-covenant position.

How can you make the celebration of Communion a bigger part of your worship with God?

Are You Experiencing an Identity Crisis?

Before they fought for their inheritance, the Israelites set up camp at Gilgal. They circumcised the males and celebrated Passover together. I believe that baptism and Communion are two of the ways we can "set up camp" to help us remember the blessings of the new covenant. Baptism and Communion point to our new-covenant identity. Are you suffering from an identity crisis?

When Justin and Josh were three and five respectively, I took them to the zoo. Running from exhibit to exhibit, the boys were having a good time identifying all the different animals. We came to one enclosure and saw several ostriches strut by us. Justin, my three-year-old, got a big smile on his face and exclaimed, "Look, Mama, look. It's a duck!" "No," I said. "That's an ostrich." Justin looked closer, put his hands on his hips, and said, "Nope. It's a duck!"

Josh and I could not help but laugh. Josh tried to convince his little brother, but to no avail. Justin, stubborn as his mama, continued to believe that what he saw was a duck. Josh and I gave up and we moved on. Justin left there that day holding fast to his belief that ducks were five feet tall with long necks and fluffy feathers on their back.

You can be a Christian and still struggle with your identity in Christ. Although God sees you as a new creation and in complete right standing with him, you may, like Justin, believe something completely different. Our actions will always follow our belief system. Remember your new identity through baptism and Communion. Christ, your Passover lamb, has been sacrificed. His blood of the new covenant was poured out for the forgiveness of your sins. You have been raised to new life.

Your New Identity Is in Jesus

After the Israelites crossed over the Jordan River, the manna went away and they ate the fruit of the land. Take another look, a good look, at your new-covenant position in Christ. The same Holy Spirit that filled the early church is on the King's table. You are not a duck or an ostrich. Your new identity is in Christ. In Christ, you are God's child. The power and penalty of sin have been destroyed. God has made you an eagle … and you are meant to fly (Isaiah 40:31).

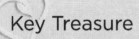

Key Treasure

Christianity that requires courage, rather than Christianity that demands comfort, requires you to stand in the New-Covenant strength that only God can provide.

Chapter 5
GOING THROUGH THE WALL

My nourish notes for Joshua 5:12–6:27

Day 1: Reveal

Meditate on the scriptures, prayerfully reading and reflecting on the verses. Mark the phrases, verses, or words that catch your attention. Journal and learn more as the Lord leads you.

Day 2: Respond

Respond to activate truth in your life. The **IMPACT** acronym provides questions to help you apply the Word. Sometimes you may not have an answer to all six questions.

Image of God to trust? *An attribute of God, Jesus, or the Holy Spirit to trust.*

Message to share? *A word of encouragement, truth, or a prayer to share with others.*

Promise to treasure? *A promise in the Bible to stand on by faith.*

Action to take? *A specific step God is calling you to take.*

Core authentic identity to embrace? *A truth about how God sees you to agree with in your heart.*

Transgression to confess or forgive? *A confession to receive healing, help, and restoration through Christ.*

Day 3: Renew

Carry God's Word with you during the week. Renew your mind daily by focusing on one word, verse, or truth that the Holy Spirit revealed through the Bible. Like an anchor that secures its vessel, renewing your mind with the truth brings security and focus, despite the waves you face during the day.

My Anchor of Truth:

NOURISH JOURNAL

Additional space to record any further thoughts God has shared with me.

DAY 4

Join with me in suffering, like a good soldier of Christ Jesus.
—2 Timothy 2:3

The preparations were complete. Joshua crossed the Jordan River leading the Israelites to this one defining moment. God was about to prove himself as their strength through a battle fought with spiritual weapons—the sound of trumpets, praise, and simple faith.

The Israelites' inheritance was secure, but they still had to fight battles in the Promised Land. You are secure in Christ the moment you become a Christian, but the battle for your soul—your mind, will, and emotions—has only just begun. The enemy knows that your eternal inheritance as a child of God is secure, but he can tempt you to act independently from God. As much as there is a God who loves you and wants to give you abundant life, there is also an enemy who wants to wreak havoc in your life (John 10:10).

One of Satan's much-used tools of deception involves convincing you to depend on yourself … or on other people … or on power or wealth—anything but God. He tells you that if you are going to win the battles of life, you have to do it on your own.

We don't have to fight on our own. We can choose to depend on Jesus. In the wilderness Moses told Joshua that God would fight *for* them to give them victory (Deuteronomy 1:30; 20:4). In the battle to submit your mind, will, and emotions to God you *can* lean on *his* strength and not depend on your own. God wants you to enter all battles as Joshua did—with spiritual weapons.

Why?

Why did Joshua have to fight so many battles? Why couldn't the Israelites defeat all the enemies in one swoop, claim their inheritance, and live at peace?

Why do we have to fight battles? Why do Christians suffer pain? Why is our sanctification a process instead of an instant purification? Why the heartache? Christians throughout the years have written many books on these subjects, and still we are left with "Why?"

We can, however, glean some truths from the Scriptures that give us hope in the midst of our heartache. Our temporary home on earth is a fallen world (John 16:33). None of us are immune to the ramifications of a world that chooses to live independently of God (Romans 3:23). The curse of sin affects us all. Evil, sickness, depression, hate, and famine are not from God. In heaven suffering and evil will cease (Revelation 21:4); but for now, we live in a fallen world.

God Can Bring Good from Every Battle

God will bring good out of every battle (Romans 8:28). God wants to help us through all battles large and small: the trials we face externally, and the struggles we have internally. Battles teach us how to fight spiritually (Judges 3:2). God uses hardship to prune us (John 15:2). Troubles increase our compassion so that we are better able to comfort others (2 Corinthians 1:3–4). Suffering brings us closer to Christ (Romans 8:15–17).

As each challenge compels us to press into God, we experience how he fights for us. If we never faced any difficulties in life, how would we ever know Christ as our deliverer? Facing temptation helps us know him as our rescuer. Facing insecurity leads us to know that Christ is our identity. Struggling with sin draws us to Christ as our redeemer. Being in a place of need reveals God as provider. And on and on it goes. If we press into Christ during hard times, we learn that we can depend on God for everything we need.

Keep Your Eyes on Jesus … Not the Circumstances

When Joshua was near Jericho, he looked up and saw the commander of the Lord's army. Jericho was tightly shut up (Joshua 6:1) with walls "to the sky" shielding people stronger and taller than the Israelites (Deuteronomy 1:28). It would have been easy for Joshua to view the magnitude of his enemies, and then look back yearningly at the wilderness where the battles had been few. But Joshua chose to look up … and he found his strength in the commander of the Lord's army.

Scholars have differing opinions about the identity of the commander of the Lord's army. Some interpretations conclude that the man Joshua saw was an angel, while other scholars say that he was Jesus. I believe the man was Christ because Joshua bowed down before him. Throughout the Bible, angels never allowed others to worship them (Daniel 10:10; Revelation 19:10). You may want to check out several commentaries, but for our purposes, I am speaking from the standpoint that the commander of the Lord's army is Christ.

Like Joshua, we can fix our eyes on Jesus to find our strength or we can focus on the distractions, which deplete us. If we don't look to Jesus for the answer and trust his strength rather than our own, the enemy will be able to pull us back into our old ways. Or we might passively pull away from the battle because we think we are helpless in our circumstances.

Proverbs 4:25–27 says, "Keep your eyes straight ahead; ignore all sideshow distractions. Watch your step, and the road will stretch out smooth before you. Look neither right nor left; leave evil in the dust" (MSG). The enemy knows he can stop us, but he cannot stop Jesus. Jesus is the Lamb of God who takes away our sins, but he is also the Lion of Judah, the commander of the Lord's army, ready and willing to fight for you. Keep your eyes on Jesus and leave evil in the dust.

Good Soldiers Follow Their Commander

If Jesus is the commander of the Lord's army, that makes us his soldiers. Why else would God give us his armor or tell us to fight the good fight (Ephesians 6:10–18; 1Timothy 6:12)?

Our Commander calls us to fight our battles God's way. "Join with me in suffering, like a good soldier of Christ Jesus. No one serving as a soldier gets entangled in civilian affairs, but rather tries to please his commanding officer. Similarly, anyone who competes as an athlete does not receive the victor's crown except by competing according to the rules" (2 Timothy 2:3–5).

What are God's ways? Ask Jesus, your commander, for a battle plan and follow it. Use your spiritual weapons, and know that as you trust in the Lion of Judah, he is fighting for you. Don't run away. Don't use earthly weapons, even to accomplish godly purposes. Earthly weapons can be anything from vengeance, to manipulation, to gossip, to flattery. No matter how godly our goals are, God calls us to play by his rules and trust him. Spiritual weapons include prayer, the armor of God, obedience, forgiveness, the fullness of the Holy Spirit, speaking the Word, and, most importantly, love. Stand firm and fight God's way until love wins over hate.

Jesus Forgives All

"Joshua went up to him and asked, 'Are you for us or for our enemies?' 'Neither,' he replied, 'but as commander of the army of the LORD I have now come'" (Joshua 5:13–14). I believe that Scripture points to the fact that Jesus is for all; he is always ready to forgive anyone, even our enemies. Jesus came to save the world (John 3:16–17). Jesus calls us to forgive our enemies also (Matthew 6:12–15).

Forgiveness is one of the most powerful weapons of spiritual warfare. Forgiveness is not a feeling—it is a choice. Unforgiveness keeps us in a prison. Forgiveness is freedom and healing. Forgiveness does not mean saying that the wrong someone did was right. Forgiveness does not mean necessarily trusting your offender again. Forgiveness is releasing the person to God for him to work in his or her life.

It is healthy and necessary to draw boundaries with people if we are in danger. However, God calls us to rise up against evil, not against people acting in evil ways.

Revenge does nothing for you because you are fighting the wrong enemy. Our struggles are not against flesh and blood but against the spiritual forces of evil in the heavenly realms (Ephesians 6:12). God is the just judge. Vengeance is his (Romans 12:19). He will rescue you (Psalm 18:48). Instead of lashing out at people, take the anger you feel and pour it out against the real enemy—Satan. Fighting spiritually moves mountains. Get behind the Lord and watch him fight on your behalf as you walk in forgiveness and love.

Face the Battle with a Brave Heart

Joshua's reaction to the seemingly impossible battle before him was not to run away, but to press into the Lord. Joshua faced the battle with obedience. Even though Joshua had been exalted in the eyes of the Israelites … even though the Lord had granted him this position of leadership … even though he was getting ready to face possible death … Joshua bowed down before Jesus and said, "What orders does my Master have for his *servant*?" (Joshua 5:14 MSG, *emphasis mine*).

The wilderness was a relatively peaceful place without many battles. It's a different story in the Promised Land. When we press forward into the Promised Land, we can expect battles. As a servant and joint heir of Christ, "we share in his sufferings in order that we may also share in his glory" (Romans 8:17).

How do you respond to challenges, battles, and difficulties in life?

_____

_____

_____

_____

Joshua responded by embracing the battle. He pressed onward to overcome his enemies with faith in God's promise of the inheritance. He bowed down before the commander of the Lord's army, committing to follow his battle plan. He identified himself as a servant (Joshua 5:14) and walked humbly before God and man.

Second Chronicles 7:14 says, "If my people, who are called by my name, will humble themselves and pray and seek my face and turn from their wicked ways, then I will hear from heaven, and I will forgive their sin and will heal their land." Healing occurs when we stop wrestling God and become his servant.

With the Lion of Judah on your side, you have his power and strength working on your behalf. You can submit to God and the devil will flee (James 4:7). In the heat of overwhelming circumstances, look up. The commander of the Lord's army is ready to fight for you.

We can spend a lifetime asking "why" and running away … or we can surrender to be the Lord's servant no matter what the cost, knowing that the Lion of Judah is all the strength we need. When we trust the Great Shepherd enough to walk humbly by his side, we walk in the shadow of his strength to do great things for him. This surrender to God's perfect love is what becoming a *brave heart* is all about.

DAY 5

One who is wise can go up against the city of the mighty
and pull down the stronghold in which they trust.
—*Proverbs 21:22*

Jericho was a mighty city, a stronghold with securely shut walls reaching toward the sky. In fact, some archaeological evidence suggests that there were actually two walls around the city. Webster's Dictionary defines *stronghold* as a fortified place of security.

Another Kind of Stronghold

Strongholds can also exist in our minds. A stronghold in our minds is any thinking opposed to God's truth. Just as Joshua had to tear down the stronghold of Jericho first to experience victory in the Promised Land, tearing down the strongholds in our minds must be a priority to experience victory in our Christian walk.

Your thinking affects your actions. When your thinking aligns with the Word of God, your actions will submit to the Spirit of God. When you became a Christian, you became a new creation, but your thinking was still shaped by your past experiences. Past hurts and worldly views leave dents in our souls that push us to get our needs met without God. Consequently, these strongholds cause many Christians to continue to live in defeat.

We will continue to struggle with sin unless we tear down our old strongholds by changing the way we think. The Greek word for stronghold is *ochyroma*, which means a fortress or anything on which one relies.[1] After we become Christians, we have a wonderful opportunity for God to be our refuge, trust, and stronghold. However, our natural instincts, ingrained in our minds from our past, corrupt our actions. Even after we become Christians, all kinds of forces play out in our lives that cause us to try to face our challenges our own way, independent of God. The world has a multitude of names for these forces: defense mechanisms, self-made success, addictions, lifestyles ... and on and on. God calls them strongholds.

Overcoming Strongholds in Your Life

A stronghold can be difficult to identify because over a period of time the behavior becomes so natural that we are blind to the error. We react in ways contrary to God's Word but don't think we are doing anything wrong because it "feels right."

God gave me a great illustration of overcoming strongholds on the ski slopes. (Yes, on the ski slopes. God speaks to us everywhere!) After my instructor observed me ski one run, he said, "Aliene, when you turn, you are leaning up the mountain instead of bowing to the valley. If you lean downhill instead of uphill when you turn, your weight will be on the correct foot and your skis will turn naturally."

He then took me to an easy slope so I could practice bowing to the valley instead of leaning up the hill. At every turn I would say to myself, "Bow to the valley." My weight shifted correctly and my skis naturally turned. It worked!

When we met at the bottom of the hill, my instructor explained that it is a natural instinct to lean up the mountain to keep from falling. "You have skied this way for years," he said. "It will be hard to break, but once you change your thinking that leaning down the mountain will keep you from falling, you're home free."

We stayed on the beginner slopes and my skiing was smooth. It was easy to remember to "bow to the valley." However, the first time we tried a more challenging slope, I was scared and reverted to my old way of leaning up the hill. Although I could hear my instructor yelling, "Bow to the valley, bow to the valley!" I continued to depend on my old way of thinking and I fell. Starting down the hill a second time, I said aloud, "Bow to the valley; bow to the valley," and it worked! The more I skied relying on my new way of thinking, the more bowing to the valley became my natural response.

Transformation

If you want your actions to line up with Christ so that your life reflects his, you must retrain the way you think by tearing down your strongholds. "Do not conform to the pattern of this world, but be transformed by the renewing of your mind. Then you will be able to test and approve what God's will is—his good, pleasing and perfect will" (Romans 12:2).

It is not enough to cover up your jealousy, anger, or bitterness with a smile. You must allow Christ to heal the root issue. Transformation comes from within. "The weapons we fight with are not the weapons of the world. On the contrary, they have divine power to demolish strongholds. We demolish arguments and every pretension that sets itself up against the knowledge of God, and we take captive every thought to make it obedient to Christ" (2 Corinthians 10:4–5).

Any thought that sets itself up against Christ must go. And we can tear it down not by striving to be better, but by using spiritual weapons. Ultimately, the Lord identifies strongholds in our lives. Joshua fell facedown and asked God what he should do, and you must do the same. The first step is to pray and ask God to reveal strongholds in your life.

You can use God's Word to take your "stronghold temperature." The Word is a mirror reflecting the areas of your life that do—and don't—line up with God's will. Repeated sin could be the sign of a stronghold. It is not about feeling condemned—it is about getting to the root of the issue.

> Start with Galatians 5:16–25. Take a look at the acts of the flesh. With which ones do you struggle?

Identifying and Overcoming Strongholds

Anger is one of my struggles. Whenever I feel like having a "fit of rage," or saying something passive-aggressive; I know there is a pattern of thinking against God's truth in his Word. For example, I was getting angry when my house, my life, my kids, my husband, or I was not perfect. The anger was the result of a stronghold in my thoughts that said, "You are not valuable unless you are perfect. Other people expect you to be perfect. Life has to be fair, perfect, and comfortable for you to be happy."

That thinking sets itself up against God's truth. Christ is my perfection. God loves me for who I am. I can be myself, weaknesses and all, around others. Right thinking yields right living. The more my thinking lines up with this truth, the more my frustration subsides.

Whenever you are tempted to act out in the flesh, you should recognize that your stronghold temperature is high because you are trying to get your needs met without God, to do things your way instead of his. The next time you are tempted to act out in the flesh, begin to journal your thoughts to God. Ask him to reveal the stronghold or line of thinking that is causing you to follow your flesh instead of being led by the Spirit. There may be walls that have been in your life for so long that you don't recognize them at first. As you seek God for the truth, you will begin to see a pattern that has developed in your thinking that sets itself up against the way God wants you to think.

God helped Joshua identify Jericho as a stronghold to attack, and then he gave him the battle plan to tear the walls down. Pray, read the Word, and allow the Holy Spirit to lead you to recognize your individual strongholds. Identifying wrong patterns of thinking is absolutely necessary to walk out your freedom in Christ.

I want to close this day with a story I wrote to encourage you to identify the strongholds in your own life … and trust in the Great Shepherd.

The Great Shepherd

Once upon a time, a little lamb lived in the flock of the Great Shepherd. The Great Shepherd loved the little lamb. She was his pride and joy. She had many gifts and unique abilities, and the Great Shepherd delighted in watching her grow. That is how the Great Shepherd felt about all of his flock. But that is not the way the little lamb felt about herself.

As much as the Great Shepherd loved her, other voices said just the opposite. "You are insignificant," she would hear. "You're ugly. You're no good. You'll never amount to anything. You're not worth much. You're a failure. You can't do anything right."

Unfortunately, the little lamb heard these voices from other sheep in the flock. The Great Shepherd's heart broke from seeing her in so much pain. As the years passed, the voices continued and made a permanent impression in her mind. The negative thoughts became a part of her own thinking whether or not someone was saying them at the time.

Although the Great Shepherd continued to tell her how wonderful he thought she was, the lamb believed the voices in her head. The more she believed the voices, the more they became real to her.

The Great Shepherd stood and called for his little lamb. He longed to rescue her, but the little lamb was filled with shame and so she did not feel worthy to come to the Great Shepherd when he called. Trying to get rid of the pain, she turned and ran away. Sometimes the accusing voices would confuse her, and she even thought that perhaps they were from the Great Shepherd himself. And so she ran away again and again to escape the voices. But no matter where she hid, the voices would always find her.

The Great Shepherd continued to call her name. "Beautiful, beloved, where are you? I long to tell you how special you are."

But the little lamb was confused and believed the voices over the truth of the Great Shepherd. One day the voices were so strong that they were not just a whisper in her head but a loud shout: "Lamb, lamb, run away. Hurry! You're too much of a failure for the Great Shepherd to ever use you. Run away!"

So the little lamb ran away, but the voices became even louder and stronger. "See the cliff over there, little lamb? Run and jump! Then the voices will end forever. Then you will not be a burden to any of the other sheep and most of all, the Great Shepherd."

And so the little lamb ran and ran, and she saw the cliff the voices had told her about. She took a deep breath, closed her eyes, and, desperately wanting to silence the voices, she jumped off the cliff.

But the voices had lied to her again. She had not escaped them. When she jumped, she broke bones in her legs and couldn't run anymore. The voices immediately returned. "What a failure. I can't believe you did this. You are terrible! The Great Shepherd will never talk to you now. And you can't run. You are trapped."

Many sheep came to see the lamb and looked sadly on her life. Some even believed that she had given up, but not the Great Shepherd.

The Great Shepherd had other plans. He picked up the little broken lamb and placed her securely around his neck and across his shoulders with her legs on either side of his head. At first, the little lamb squirmed to escape because she had developed a natural instinct to run away. She was afraid the Great Shepherd would not love her.

But because of her broken body, she was unable to run and was forced to rest across the shoulders of the Great Shepherd. Little by little, she began to trust him.

She was so close to the Great Shepherd she could hear him saying, "Little lamb, I love you. I am so sorry this happened. You are so beautiful and so valuable. You are so significant and important to me." The little lamb heard the Great Shepherd, and she wanted to believe him. But still she heard the other voices.

The little lamb asked the Great Shepherd about this one day. The Great Shepherd taught her that she had the authority in his name to tell the voices to leave. Then he reached out and scratched her behind her ears and said,"Then, you must choose to believe that what I say about you is true." And so the little lamb told the voices to leave in the Great Shepherd's name. And then she began to believe what the Great Shepherd said about her. She used her own voice to repeat what the Great Shepherd would tell her, and slowly but surely her thinking changed. She began to see herself as a beautiful, divine creation. And the voices were gone.

While the little lamb was on the Shepherd's back, she did not have the choice to run anymore. And so the little lamb learned she could trust the Great Shepherd for everything. Because her body was broken, she learned that the Great Shepherd was her healer. Because she didn't have the ability to get food for herself, she learned that she could trust the Great Shepherd to provide for her. Because she could not protect herself when they walked through the valleys, she learned that the Great Shepherd was her protector. As she rested securely between his shoulders, she learned that the Great Shepherd was her peace. Because she was too weak to walk, she learned that the Great Shepherd was her strength. Because he rescued her and put her securely across his shoulders, she learned that the Great Shepherd loved her unconditionally and was the source of her redemption and forgiveness.

One day the little lamb realized that she could find everything she ever needed in the Great Shepherd. She knew she could trust him and did not have to run away anymore. She realized that his voice was the truth, and she wanted to stay right by his side and follow him. She was ready to trust.

The Great Shepherd took her off his shoulders and placed her firmly on the ground. The lamb was healed and could not only walk, but also run. But because of what the Great Shepherd had taught her on his shoulders, she chose to walk humbly by his side. She knew she could trust the Great Shepherd for everything that she needed. She also knew that she was a beautiful, divine creation. Many times the Great Shepherd would ask her to do important things for him.

And so she followed the Great Shepherd the rest of her days even though her life was not perfect. She walked with a limp. However, she was very proud of her imperfection because it gave her the opportunity to tell other little lambs in the flock how amazing the Great Shepherd really is. Her imperfection and weakness also kept her leaning and resting on the strength of the Great Shepherd. Even when they walk through the valleys during difficult times, she is right by his side. The little lamb has become a sheep. She calls herself beautiful, and the Great Shepherd smiles.

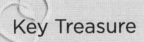

Key Treasure

When your thinking aligns with the Word of God, your actions will submit to the Spirit of God.

DAY 6

When the trumpets sounded, the army shouted, and at the sound of the trumpet, when the men gave a loud shout, the wall collapsed; so everyone charged straight in, and they took the city. They devoted the city to the Lord and destroyed with the sword every living thing in it—men and women, young and old, cattle, sheep and donkeys. —*Joshua 6:20–21*

Joshua's mind must have been filled with the image of those high, thick walls of Jericho. He had seen the walls himself and heard the spies' report. I wonder if he thought, *How are we going to conquer this one, Lord? I am mighty with my sword, and I know you were faithful to pull back those waters of the Jordan as you did in the Red Sea. But walls? This challenge seems bigger than I am.*

Perhaps that is how you feel about your strongholds. The good news of the gospel is that all things are possible through Christ (Philippians 4:13). Change *is* possible. His strength is always more than enough.

Choose God's Way

Whatever strongholds you are facing, God will help you tear them down ... but you must use spiritual weapons. If you have faith in God's way of fighting strongholds, you will use his methods and win. It took faith for the Israelites to pick up trumpets instead of weapons. But they chose to do it God's way—and he gave them the victory. "By faith the walls of Jericho fell, after the army had marched around them for seven days" (Hebrews 11:30).

In order to tear down a stronghold, you cannot run away from it, suppress it, or ignore it. You have to deal with it—God's way. "For though we live in the world, we do not wage war as the world does. The weapons we fight with are not the weapons of the world. On the contrary, they have divine power to demolish strongholds" (2 Corinthians 10:3–4).

Spiritual Vision

The first command God gave Joshua was to change his thinking. What Joshua saw with his earthly eyes was a heavily guarded city and a trained army of strong fighting men. But the Lord asked him to see it with spiritual eyes. "See, I have delivered Jericho into your hands" (Joshua 6:2).

Ask God for spiritual vision in order that you might see the truth in your situation. As you study the Word ask the Holy Spirit to show you any line of thinking that sets itself up against the knowledge of God. Change the way you think by meditating on scriptures that reveal truth.

Verbally renounce the lies that have deceived you and speak the truth of the scriptures. For example, when I am dealing with perfectionism, I might say, "I renounce the lie that I have to be perfect, and I accept the truth that I am fearfully and wonderfully made and God loves me just the way I am." The more you meditate on the truth in God's Word, the more your thinking will change.

We all have wounds in our souls that need God's healing. When I was fourteen, something happened in my life that hurt me greatly. To handle the pain, I made an inner vow to depend only on myself so that I would never get hurt again. This resolve to be strong set up a stronghold of thinking against the knowledge that God is my strength. I made a subconscious agreement with the enemy that I could not depend on God to rescue me. I went elsewhere to find my strength. This, of course, left me tired, defeated, and disappointed with others.

God heard my cries and helped me see the truth. Through the book of Psalms, I discovered many scriptures assuring me that God alone is my strength and that I can trust him. The Lord showed me I had left no room for him to rescue me because I continually chose to depend on myself. As I began to renounce the lies and meditate on the truth, my actions began to change.

I do not *have* to get angry with others or take matters into my own hands. As God gives me the grace to see with spiritual eyes, I am able to walk in a new freedom of peace and trust.

Brick by brick, my wall is coming down. Do I still have times when I struggle? You bet. However, the more I am able to apply these truths, the easier it is to recognize when this is happening again.

The more we experience victory by seeing our lives through the eyes of Christ, the more we have faith that God's Word is a powerful spiritual weapon to tear down any stronghold.

Praise and Worship

Another spiritual weapon against strongholds is praise and worship. God instructed the Israelites to march around Jericho and sound the trumpets for six days. On the seventh day, they were to give a shout. In the Old Testament, trumpets were used to praise God, announce a battle, and call an assembly (Numbers 10:2–10; Psalm 98:6, 150:3). Trumpets were used to make Jericho's walls fall. Your worship and praise can make the walls of your stronghold fall as well.

When we choose to worship God, he reveals his character to us repeatedly. Worship is thanking God for who he is, and praise is thanking God for what he has done. Worship is another way to meditate on his character. Praise will give you a heavenly perspective on your situation. Worship and praise get your mouth and your thinking off your circumstances and in line with God. Praise and worship announce to the enemy that you are aligning yourself with the Lord. It's your victory cry!

Worship helps us make God our stronghold. The more we meditate on who God is through praise and worship, the easier it is for us to trust him. When we trust him, other strongholds fade away. David said, "Those who know your name trust in you, for you, LORD, have never forsaken those who seek you" (Psalm 9:10). "The name of the LORD is a fortified tower; the righteous run to it and are safe" (Proverbs 18:10).

I wonder if any of the Israelites thought, "God, you must be crazy. Blowing trumpets to tear down those walls? Impossible!" But they followed God with their whole hearts, and the walls fell. Perhaps you think praise and worship cannot tear down the walls in your own life. Think again through the eyes of faith.

The next time you are tempted to walk in the ways of the flesh, stop and praise God. Get your praise music cranking. Sing your favorite worship songs at the top of your lungs. Meditate on the names of God. Read a psalm aloud. Speak out the name of Jesus.

Often I am tempted to stop fighting God's way and take matters into my own hands when I don't see my walls fall right away. You might find yourself feeling the same way, but I encourage you to be persistent! The Israelites continued to follow God's plan of attack even though the walls did not immediately fall. In our instant gratification culture, I am afraid I have been conditioned to expect immediate results. But God's ways often require patient obedience. For seven days or seven years, "let us not become weary in doing good, for at the proper time we will reap a harvest if we do not give up" (Galatians 6:9).

An On-Going Process

On the seventh day, the harvest came: the walls came down with a shout from the Israelites! But that is not the end of the story.

Joshua told the Israelites to destroy everything in the city except items designated for the Lord's treasury. They were not to keep any of the things set for destruction. The Israelites went in and destroyed the city completely with the sword. Joshua stood over the ruins of the city and pronounced, "Cursed before the LORD is the one who undertakes to rebuild this city, Jericho" (Joshua 6:26).

After a spiritual victory the enemy can tempt you to return to your old ways and rebuild the stronghold. Don't feel guilty if you feel like returning to your old ways. Child of God, you are not defeated because of the way you feel. Replace your feelings with faith.

How do we do this? We can't change the way we feel without asking God's help through prayer. Anytime we are tempted to go back to our stronghold, we must use our sword of the Spirit, which is the Word of God (Ephesians 6:17). The Israelites destroyed the city with the sword. Memorize scriptures and speak them aloud anytime temptation comes. All you need is one Scripture. Hang on to it for dear life, if need be. Through the Holy Spirit devote your mind (Philippians 4:8–9) and your mouth (1 Corinthians 6:19–20) to the Lord and don't ever turn back.

If we have forgiven someone, we must resolve not to go back and pick up bitterness. If we have released manipulation, we must resist trying to control others and instead trust that God is in control. If we have torn down the walls of escape, we can resist using food, fantasies, alcohol, or shopping and instead turn to God. If we have walked away from worry, we can continue trusting God. If we have walked away from excess, we must resolve to have balance.

God as Our Stronghold

We have a choice. We can trust our stronghold, or we can trust in the Great Shepherd as our security. Yes, mighty warriors, there will be battles in the Promised Land. But praise God, he has given us the spiritual weapons to identify and tear down our strongholds one by one!

Realize your strongholds with God's help. **Realign** your thinking with God's Word. **Recognize** and **renounce** the lies you believe. **Ring** your trumpets of worship and praise. **Resist** rebuilding your stronghold through Christ.

What are some of your strongholds? What Scripture can you find to help you realign your thinking with God's Word? In closing, take some time to pray using your spiritual weapons of God's Word, worship, and praise.

Demolish your walls and defeat your enemies God's way. Keep your sword of the Spirit handy; the next battle is around the corner.

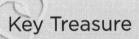

Key Treasure

Realize your strongholds with God's help. Realign your thinking with God's Word. Recognize and renounce the lies you believe. Ring your trumpets of worship and praise. Resist rebuilding your stronghold through Christ.

Chapter 6
BLESSED ASSURANCE

My nourish notes for Joshua 7-8

Day 1: Reveal

Meditate on the scriptures, prayerfully reading and reflecting on the verses. Mark the phrases, verses, or words that catch your attention. Journal and learn more as the Lord leads you.

Day 2: Respond

Respond to activate truth in your life. The **IMPACT** acronym provides questions to help you apply the Word. Sometimes you may not have an answer to all six questions.

Image of God to trust? *An attribute of God, Jesus, or the Holy Spirit to trust.*

Message to share? *A word of encouragement, truth, or a prayer to share with others.*

Promise to treasure? *A promise in the Bible to stand on by faith.*

Action to take? *A specific step God is calling you to take.*

Core authentic identity to embrace? *A truth about how God sees you to agree with in your heart.*

Transgression to confess or forgive? *A confession to receive healing, help, and restoration through Christ.*

Day 3: Renew

Carry God's Word with you during the week. Renew your mind daily by focusing on one word, verse, or truth that the Holy Spirit revealed through the Bible. Like an anchor that secures its vessel, renewing your mind with the truth brings security and focus, despite the waves you face during the day.

My Anchor of Truth:

NOURISH JOURNAL

Additional space to record any further thoughts God has shared with me.

DAY 4

For it is by grace you have been saved, through faith—
and this not from yourselves, it is the gift of God.
—*Ephesians 2:8*

Up until this point Joshua and the Israelites saw victory and success as the Lord had promised in the beginning of their quest (Joshua 1:7–8). Things had gone well, *but* … "But the Israelites were unfaithful in regard to the devoted things" (Joshua 7:1). In blatant disobedience to God's instructions, Achan chose to turn, look at the riches, and covet.

God claimed the riches of Jericho, the first fruits, as devoted to him alone. *But*, led by selfish desires, Achan took the devoted things, an act of sin that led to Israel's first defeat. At first, Joshua was unaware of this trespass because Achan hid the spoils under his tent. *But* nothing is ever hidden from God, not even the "secrets" buried in our hearts.

Uprooting the Sin

The effects of sin are devastating. Sin does not affect just you—it hurts your family, your friends, and the body of Christ. Achan's sin was buried in the family tent. The family kept a terrible secret that would ultimately lead to their death. Joshua 7:1 says the *Israelites* committed a sin. Achan's hypocrisy affected all the Israelites. Likewise, the church suffers as a whole when we sin.

Not following God also gives an open door to the enemy to wreak havoc in our lives (Ephesians 4:27). At Ai, Israel saw defeat for the first time because of Achan's selfishness and disobedience.

Joshua fell flat on his face, crying out to God. This time he bowed, not to worship, but to ask why Israel had experienced defeat. God revealed to him that Israel sinned and would not be able to stand before their enemies until they destroyed the accursed thing (Joshua 7:10–13). In other words, before they could again be victorious in battle, the hidden sin would need to be exposed and pulled out by the root.

The same is true with us. If we do not deal with the root issues of our sin, we will never walk in victory. We sin. We feel guilty and those feelings of condemnation compel us to hide our sin. We have two choices at this point: depend on ourselves, cover the sin and hide in shame … or … depend on God's grace and take the sin to Christ and allow his grace to heal us.

Pride and Selfishness Motivate Us to Sin

Sin in Hebrew actually means to miss the mark.[1] When we sin, we step off the path or the mark God has set for us to walk.

Sin is motivated by pride and selfishness. Selfishness and pride say, *I don't need you, God. I am going to get my needs met my way. I am going to trust myself to get the job done. My way is better, God, and I am not willing to depend on you.*

Proverbs 16:18 tells us that pride comes before we fall. Pride does not leave any room for God to work (Psalm 10:4). It was prideful for Joshua not to inquire of the Lord before he sent the troops off to battle. It was selfish for Achan to follow his own way instead of God's, and take the spoils for himself. He thought he knew a better way than God's plan. This is also pride.

Usually our pride and selfishness stem from past hurts. The name Achan means "troubler." Although we do not know specifics about Achan's past, we know that he heard his name "troubler" over and over again. Negative words spoken over us wound us, and leave scars.

Past hurts push us to depend on ourselves instead of God, which leads to pride and selfishness. Instead of living like a child of God, we live like an orphan trying to get our needs met by expecting others to do it for us or by depending on our own methods. A selfish, prideful desire rises up to take what Christ has already died to give us. Instead of resting in the Father's arms, we are striving and depending on our own self efforts to feel significant, secure, and loved.

Grace Is the Answer

Grace is the answer to our selfishness. When you understand God's grace and love for YOU personally, selfishness melts away because you realize you can trust God to meet all your needs. Your heavenly Father cares about every detail of your life and longs to give you the desires of your heart as you delight yourself in him (Psalm 37:4).

The closer we walk with Jesus, the more we must depend on him. Joshua fell on his face before the Lord and once again declared his dependence on God. Achan's response was to depend on himself by hiding his trespass. Joshua found redemption, Achan reaped destruction.

The Pattern of Sin

Achan's confession tells us a lot about how the law stirs up our desire to sin. God commanded the Israelites when they defeated Jericho, "... keep away from the devoted things,... All the silver and gold and the articles of bronze and iron are sacred to the LORD and must go into his treasury" (Joshua 6:18–19). Paul says that while the law is good and holy, it actually stirs up the sin nature inside of us (Romans 7:7–17).In other words, like a child, when we hear *keep away*, we naturally want to *run to*.

Achan's sin nature resulted in an act of disobedience spurred on by greed. He confessed, "When I saw in the plunder a beautiful robe from Babylonia, two hundred shekels of silver and a bar of gold weighing fifty shekels, I coveted them and took them. They are hidden in the ground inside my tent, with the silver underneath" (Joshua 7:21). He **saw**, he **coveted**, he **took**, and he **hid** his sin. The pattern for Achan's sin mirrors the original sin in the garden of Eden. God told Adam and Eve not to eat from the tree of knowledge of good and evil. Eve **saw** the fruit, **wanted** it, **took** it, and then **hid** from the Lord (Genesis 3:2–8). We see. We want. We sin. We hide in shame.

Although the expression of sin may have different flavors, the pattern of sin remains the same. Guilt and shame cause us to hide our mistakes instead of taking them to God for redemption.

We See

Just like Achan, whatever we look at can open up the doors for temptation. Jesus said, "The eye is the lamp of the body. If your eyes are healthy, your whole body will be full of light. But if your eyes are unhealthy, your whole body will be full of darkness" (Matthew 6:22–23).

The media feeds us worldly values. Movies and books glamorize adultery. Advertisements convince us that *stuff* makes us happy and we need more. Talk show hosts push the New Age movement. Magazine covers promote perfection. Violent video games and horror movies desensitize us to violence. The Internet fills homes with pornography. Not all media is bad, but it can open up a door for the enemy to bring temptation.

We Want

Looking at things through the world's eyes instead of with a biblical perspective can lead to coveting or envy. Coveting means to desire greatly and delight in something. Coveting breeds unhappiness and depression.

Envy says, *God doesn't love me*. Nothing could be further from the truth! God blesses his children in just the right way. Peace to our souls comes when we are content with what we have and allow God to give us the desires of our heart in his way and his time.

Coveting or envy yields jealousy, greed, competition, and self-hate. Feeding these emotions wastes a lot of energy and time. The authors of *Boundaries* suggest, "Envy defines 'good' as 'what I do not possess,' and hates the good that it has.... But what is so destructive about this particular sin is that it guarantees that we will not get what we want and keeps us perpetually insatiable and dissatisfied."[2]

If Achan waited for God to provide for his needs, he could have freely taken plunder after the victory at Ai—and all with God's blessing (Joshua 8:1). Are you willing to wait for his way and his plan? He alone knows what is best for us—and he alone is able to provide it.

God can do amazing things in our lives when we trust him. Our needs are never met by our taking. In God's kingdom, our needs are met by giving (Luke 6:38). Selfishness prods us to steal what God wants to give us—if we are willing to walk patiently in obedience and to trust him.[3]

We Act; We Hide

Achan's selfishness led him to steal. The sad irony is that instead of getting to enjoy the gold, silver, and beautiful garment, he had to hide them. The draw of instant gratification to satisfy the flesh pushed Achan to disobey God, which led to shame, bondage, and ultimately death.

The devil is the father of all lies. He'll tempt you with what you see. He'll convince you that what you have is not enough. After you walk in the flesh and sin, he'll condemn you so that you will hide your sin instead of running to God to get help.

God's Love and Grace Set Us Free Through Jesus

When the hidden spoils were finally revealed, Joshua and the Israelites stoned Achan and his family to their death. Joshua knew the sin had to be destroyed for the Israelites to stand against the enemies who strived to keep them out of the Promised Land (Joshua 7:10–13).

The Bible says that the wages of sin are death (Romans 6:23). God is holy and just and so sin must be punished (1 Peter 1:15–16; 2 Thessalonians 1:6). Levitical law demands that there is no forgiveness without the shedding of blood. There can be no sin in God's presence. If that is so, who will save us from God's wrath and this meaningless way of living?

Did you know that God sent Jesus to be your Achan? Many of you have probably seen the movie *The Passion of the Christ*. As awful as his suffering was in the movie, I am told the reality of Jesus' death on the cross was far worse. Achan was stoned because of his own sin. Jesus was crucified because of ours. Why did Jesus die for sinners like us? Love. Why are we blessed beyond measure? Because of his grace.

We cannot rescue ourselves from sin. If we could cleanse ourselves of sin, then we could claim our own righteousness and Christ would have died in vain. The law does not provide the solution. We can only become a child of God through his grace (unearned favor). What the law was powerless to do in that it was weakened by the sinful nature, God did by sending his own Son in the likeness of sinful man to be a sin offering" (Romans 7:25).

In his great love, the Creator of the universe sent his Son to die in our place. Jesus paid the ultimate price for our sin. He stood in the gap by laying his life down for us. *It is because God wants us to live for him that shame and guilt were taken away on the cross.* It was because of his love for us that Jesus took the wrath of God, so that you and I could have a personal relationship with him. Our sin has been nailed to the cross. We are free from the curse of the law. The blood of Jesus covers us from the wrath of God.

The old covenant law required the priests to sacrifice lambs without defect to take away sin. Repeatedly, priests would offer these sacrifices. But Christ, our blameless Lamb of God and Great High Priest, came to sacrifice himself to redeem us from sin once and for all. And when he finished, he sat down at the right hand of the Father. Jesus sat down because the work was finished and our sin debt was paid in full (Hebrews 9–10).

God knew that we would never have our Promised Land, our spiritual inheritance, with the penalty and power of sin in our lives. He has provided a way to have freedom from your sin through Christ.

Jesus has done his part on the cross, but we must receive his grace by faith (Ephesians 2:8). How do we do this? The Bible says that when we confess with our mouths and believe in our hearts that Jesus is Lord, we are saved from the penalty and power of sin (Romans 10:8–13).

Paul, the author of two-thirds of the New Testament, expressed the struggle with sin this way: "So I find this law at work: Although I want to do good, evil is right there with me. For in my inner being I delight in God's law; but I see another law at work in me, waging war against the law of my mind and making me a prisoner of the law of sin at work within me. What a wretched man I am! Who will rescue me from this body that is subject to death?" (Romans 7:21–24). **Read the answer aloud**: "Thanks be to God—who delivers me through Jesus Christ our Lord!… Therefore, there is now no condemnation for those who are in Christ Jesus, because through Christ Jesus the law of the Spirit who gives life has set you free from the law of sin and death" (Romans 7:25–8:2).

The Bible makes it clear that grace overcomes our sin. The law is good and holy, but it has no power to free us from the attraction to sin. Romans 6:14 says, "For sin shall no longer be your master, because you are not under law, but under grace." Grace allows us to run to God for help, instead of hiding in shame.

Dealing with sin allows God to remove the root of whatever is holding us captive. The root is removed—not by our own efforts, but by receiving God's grace.

God's Love and Grace—the Only Way

Let's go to the mercy seat again in prayer and receive the Father's love. If you are not yet a Christian, make that choice right now. Choose forgiveness, choose freedom, choose life—choose Jesus.

Even if you are a Christian, you might still be living under the law, trying to bear fruit by your own efforts. Paul said to the Galatians, "I would like to learn just one thing from you: Did you receive the Spirit by the works of the law, or by believing what you heard? Are you so foolish? After beginning by means of the Spirit, are you now trying to finish by means of the flesh? Have you experienced so much in vain—if it really was in vain?" (Galatians 3:2–4). Just as we need grace for salvation, grace also gives victory over the power of sin in our lives.

Climb up into your Father's lap. He is waiting to set you free. Please pray with me.

Father, thank you for sending Jesus to die in my place. Your blood cleanses me completely and continually. Your grace is so vast I cannot understand it in my own mind. And so I come before you in simple trust to let go of my shame. I joyfully acknowledge that I cannot earn my salvation in my own ability. I acknowledge that the power of sin is taken away only by your grace. I choose to believe you today and trust in the supernatural strength of the Holy Spirit. Thank you, Jesus, for taking all of my shame. I lay it at your cross. Thank you, Jesus, for taking all the penalty of my sins—past, present, and future. I lay them at the cross. I confess you are my Lord and Savior. I thank you that I don't have to hide anymore. I will run to you for help instead of hiding because I am your child. You paid it all for me, and I give my life to you. AMEN!

DAY 5

Whoever conceals their sins does not prosper,
but the one who confesses and renounces them finds mercy.
—*Proverbs 28:13*

Last December I heard the testimony of a young woman who suffered from an eating disorder. When she came to the end of her rope, she decided to get help. During her counseling, God revealed that in her past someone sexually abused her. To deal with the pain, she had suppressed those memories until the Lord brought them to the surface. Once the truth came to light, the Lord could deal with her wounded heart, and today she no longer suffers from anorexia.

Our God is a God who restores and redeems. This is just one story among millions about the redemption of God. His light dispels the darkness through the healing hands of Christ. The young lady suffered from an eating disorder on the outside because of suppressed pain on the inside. When we invite Christ to reveal hidden hurts in our past, the light of the Lord shines in our dark closets and opens doors of hope.

Hope in Jesus

Israel suffered defeat because of Achan's spoils hidden underneath his tent. After Joshua cried out in prayer, God uncovered Israel's hidden sin and reestablished their dominion in the Promised Land, as evidenced by their victory over Ai. God redeemed them from their trouble and restored hope.

In Joshua 7:26, the Israelites named the place where they stoned Achan the Valley of Achor, which means the valley of trouble. In the future during the Tribulation, the Valley of Achor or trouble will actually become "a door of hope" and the place of rest where all Israel will be saved (Hosea 2:15; Isaiah 65:10). God can redeem any trouble or sin and restore our hope.[4]

Our hope is in the grace of Jesus Christ and our identity is in him (Colossians 1:27). To quote an old hymn "The Solid Rock," "My hope is built on nothing less than Jesus' blood and righteousness." Christ is the healer and redeemer from all sin. He makes all things new and restores hope. Under grace, given in the new covenant, there is no sin God cannot redeem.

The opposite of hope in Christ is hope in the law. When we hope to earn God's acceptance by keeping the law, the enemy can continue to accuse us because it is impossible to keep the law perfectly all the time (Galatians 2:16; Romans 3:23).

You can be a born again believer and still have an old covenant mindset. When you believe you have to earn God's forgiveness, falling into sin will naturally cause you to feel shame and hide your sin, just as Achan did (Galatians 3:1–6). The harder you try to keep the law, the more you will fail. Instead of running to Jesus for help, you will run *from* him because the enemy will remind you of your faults and condemn you.

Confession

The cross screams stop! We do not have to hide anymore. To confess means "to speak out openly." Satan wants us to remain voiceless and hiding in the dark. His tactics of condemnation motivate us to keep quiet and without help in our sin. Jesus is the only one who can heal our hurts and turn our trouble into hope. Christ fulfilled the law, so Satan cannot use our sin to condemn us! The shame is gone, in Jesus' name. We can speak freely to God and to one another. Do not hide in your shame; let the light of God's grace shine, and set you free.

Confession disarms the enemy and speaks out the truth. We are announcing to the enemy, *I am not afraid to talk to God about this problem because Jesus has paid the price for my sin yesterday, today, and tomorrow. I am completely justified. Your tactics of condemnation to keep me down in my sin do not work anymore.* Confession brings sin out into the light by bringing it to Jesus.

Confession declares our dependence on God. Confession keeps us humble and grateful for Jesus' sacrifice. Confession allows us to do something to replace our habit of hiding. Confession to one another builds our compassion. Confession breaks the silence and the hypocritical pretending because the grace that covers my sin is the same grace that covers yours. I can be real and so can you because our righteousness does not depend on following the law.

Come Out of Hiding

Read the following Scripture aloud: "Now that we know what we have—Jesus, this great High Priest with ready access to God—let's not let it slip through our fingers. We don't have a priest who is out of touch with our reality. He's been through weakness and testing, experienced it all—all but the sin. So let's walk right up to him and get what he is so ready to give. Take the mercy, accept the help" (Hebrews 4:14–16 MSG). Run to your heavenly "Abba" Father, and accept the help! When you hide, you are trying to deal with your sin through your own efforts. Our pretending, suppressing, and covering up of our sin block the healing waters of Jesus from flowing in our lives. The law promotes sin. Grace frees us from it. Grace through Jesus removes the dividing wall between God and us.

It is time to come out of hiding and go boldly before the throne of grace. Joshua fell on his face and cried out to God to find out why there was so much trouble. What is your valley of trouble?

Perhaps you are like Joshua, and someone else's hidden sin is causing destruction in your life. Maybe you missed the mark as Achan did, and instead of going to God, you are hiding because of condemnation and shame.

Just start talking to God—pour your heart out to him. Hidden sin will only fester and create more and more problems for you. The first step is to get the truth out, ask for help, and let the tears flow! What sins are buried beneath your tent? What pain have you suppressed so deeply that it is causing destruction in your life?

It is time to release the pain to God. Follow Joshua's example and take some time to ask God to shine light into the dark, hidden areas in your life. Light dispels the darkness. Ask the Holy Spirit to reveal the truth about your troubles. Take some time to pray, confess, and invite Christ in to heal your pain.

Write down what God has revealed to you.

_____

_____

_____

Journaling is a wonderful way to open up to God. Let this be the beginning of a more intimate, real relationship with God. Talk freely through prayer. Speak openly with the Lord. God will continue to reveal hidden areas that he wants to uncover and heal. It is a process of peeling away the layers. God will never give you more than you can handle. Just as Joshua had to go through layers of nation, tribes, families, and then to Achan, God will take us through the healing process through layers of his perfect timing.

Confess to One Another

God's Word says, "Confess to one another therefore your faults (your slips, your false steps, your offenses, your sins) and pray [also] for one another, that you may be healed and restored [to a spiritual tone of mind and heart]. The earnest (heartfelt, continued) prayer of a righteous man makes tremendous power available [dynamic in its working]" (James 5:16 AMPC).

Joshua said to Achan, "My son, give glory to the LORD, the God of Israel, and honor him. Tell me now what you have done; do not hide it from me" (Joshua 7:19). Confession means to speak out openly. There is something liberating that happens when we confess our sins to one another. Because of the gospel message, shame is completely gone and we can be completely real with one another. When you open up about your slips, false steps, offenses, and sins to your brothers and sisters in Christ, they can pray for you and healing and restoration begins to take place. All of us need a safe place to reveal what is hidden and find healing through prayer.

Notice the Word says that our response when someone shares is to pray with him or her. Our role is not to be Holy Spirit and figure out their issue or tell them how God solved things for us. Don't get me wrong, good sound biblical advice is not a bad thing, but the Bible calls us to pray first. You see, our advice may not be God's solution for the one in need. The ways God healed each of us may not be the ways he will heal our friends.

We are not the solution, but Christ is. Do not throw stones or judge. Mercy triumphs over judgment. Our role is to listen, love, and lead them to Christ's grace and power through prayer. Reconnect them with Christ because he is the healer and restorer of all our troubles. The power comes when we pray for our sisters and invite Christ to come in and show us how to fight the battle.

The next time someone is real about some trouble in his or her life, I challenge you to resist saying, "Here's what I would do," or "You just need to pray," or "I'll pray for you." I challenge you to remind them of God's grace and his love, and pray with that person right there on the spot.

As Christians, we all need a safe place to share our struggles without shame. It starts with each of us embracing the freedom to take off our masks. In the arms of the Father's grace, as family in Christ, we can be real with each other and find healing and restoration through Christ. We need Christ—and we need each other.

Committed, Not Flawless

After God revealed Achan's hidden sin, he commanded Joshua to consecrate himself. *Consecration* means set apart or holy. After we have failed, it is natural to feel unworthy to be set apart to serve God, but that is not the truth of the gospel. The apostle Paul never hid the fact that he had stoned and persecuted many Christians. He never felt unworthy to serve the Lord, because he knew he had been cleansed by the blood of Jesus and that it was the Holy Spirit who empowered him to do God's work. Your divorce, your depression, your disease, your dysfunction, or your downfall does not disqualify you from serving God.

Jesus is the one who makes us holy. Consecration says, *I am worthy in Christ to be set apart to follow Jesus*. It puts Jesus back on the throne. It does not mean that we are perfect; it means we are willing to follow Jesus. When we give Jesus control again after falling, he directs us to our healing, just as God gave Joshua his new battle plan.

This was not the first time God had called the Israelites to consecrate themselves. Consecration is not a onetime decision but a moment-by-moment walk of faith. Accept God's grace and move on to serve others.

When Paul came to the church at Corinth, sin was present in the camp! For example, there was jealousy, sexual immorality, and abuse of spiritual gifts. Paul did not overlook their sin, but repeatedly reminded them who they were in Christ, and that the mercy and grace of God was theirs through Christ (1 Corinthians 6:11, 15:22, 15:57; 2 Corinthians 3:3, 5:17, 5:19–20). He also encouraged them to "finish the work" (2 Corinthians 8:11), "run in such a way as to get the prize" (1 Corinthians 9:24), and to serve Christ (1 Corinthians 4:1).

Want to pursue holiness? Pursue Christ.

Power to Overcome

Sin loses it appeal when we come to Jesus and see all he did for us on the cross. "For sin shall no longer be your master, because you are not under law, but under grace" (Romans 6:14). The more we understand the grace of God, the more we will be liberated from sin. When we get a glimpse of God's mercy, we cannot help but follow him. *God's kindness leads to repentance* (Romans 2:4).

Repent in the Greek actually means to change our minds.[5] When we change our minds to line up with the truth about who we are in Christ, our actions will line up with our faith. The Word of God is the sword of the Spirit and part of the armor of God (Ephesians 6:17). Joshua *continually* held out his sword until the enemy was destroyed. When we continue to renew our minds with the gospel and grace of Christ, through speaking the Word of God, we will begin to think differently and live differently.

Jesus said, "I am the light of the world. Whoever follows me will never walk in darkness, but will have the light of life" (John 8:12).

We stop the sin cycle by following Jesus. The Bible says, "Submit yourselves, then, to God. Resist the devil, and he will flee from you" (James 4:7). Because Jesus does not condemn us, we can live in the light and be led by the Holy Spirit. Consecration brings restoration as we allow God to lead us and show us our battle plan.

You are a mighty warrior consecrated for God because you are in Christ. Jesus believes in you. The question is, do you believe it for yourself?

God Created You to Do Good Works

Grace empowers us to rise up out of our sin! The Lord said to Joshua, "Fear not nor be dismayed. Take all the men of war with you, and arise" (Joshua 8:1 AMPC). The Hebrew word for arise is *quwm* and it means to stand or to come upon the scene.[6] The enemy would love for you to continue hiding behind self-condemnation and insecurity. God needs you to come on the scene again! Arise! He has a part for you to play. You are God's handiwork, created to do good works for him (Ephesians 2:10).

The situation in the valley of Achor looked bleak. I am sure the Israelites' morale was shot after the defeat from Ai and the destruction from Achan's hidden sin. Satan would love to keep us pressed down and weighed down by all our failings, but the gospel says, *I will take all your troubles and turn them into hope.*

Hope rests in the power of the gospel message that God will take all things—even trouble we have caused—and use them for his glory. Success in God's eyes comes not from living without error, but from arising after every fall.

You have a choice today. You can continue to wallow in the shame, self-pity, self-hate, and condemnation the enemy feeds you, or you can invite God in to deal with your sin through confession. Repent and arise to receive God's grace to turn your valley of trouble into a door of hope. Get a view of God's mercy. God's grace allows you to follow God with your whole heart. Take his hand, get up out of the mud, and follow him!

Confession, repentance, and consecration dispel condemnation. Because Christ has risen, you can too. We are free to be real, we are free to boldly approach the throne of grace (not judgment!), and we are free to arise.

Key Treasure

Success in God's eyes comes not from living without error, but from arising after every fall.

DAY 6

But if you are led by the Spirit, you are not under the law.
—*Galatians 5:18*

The Israelites arose out of their defeat and came back on the scene in full force because they once again relied fully on God. Joshua did not decide how they were going to fight this time around—he allowed the Lord to lead him. This time they followed God's commands and saw his redemption. They destroyed all the inhabitants of Ai, including their king. Furthermore, God blessed the Israelites with the livestock and the spoils of the city.

Formula ... or Faith?

God wants all his children to receive and enjoy their spiritual inheritance. However, the pursuit of the Promised Land does not mean following a formula. Joshua experienced three battles, and in each one God gave him a different battle plan. In the battle with the Amalekites, the battle plan involved Moses raising his arms in prayer (Exodus 17). In Jericho, the battle plan involved playing trumpets and shouting. In the battle against Ai, God's plan involved an ambush and Joshua's javelin.

Our redemption and our healing do not come by following a formula. That is legalism. Redemption comes through the grace of Jesus Christ. Following the leading of the Spirit is being led by Jesus. Following a formula is being led by the law.

Following Jesus is not a method. It is a way of life. The battle plan to arise will be different for each person. When Christ ministered healing on earth, he told one man to put mud on his eyes, he told another to pick up his mat and walk, and another to return home because his son was healed.

Different instructions, different plans, the same Jesus.

Our Greatest Teacher

For many years, I was involved in a wonderful Bible study. In addition to attending weekly classes, I read any material I could get my hands on about the Word of God. God used teachers powerfully in my life to teach me his Word until one day when the Lord asked me to leave formal Bible study.

For about a month, I floundered around, directionless. In addition, my struggles with a particular sin were still very real. I was frustrated because I no longer had any formula to follow. *What are you doing, God? I miss my Bible teachers, and now I feel lost!*

And then God revealed to me: It was never the *Bible studies—I taught you the whole time. Now go get your Bible. Start reading Judges and I will teach you.* I picked up my Bible and a notebook and began to study, depending on the Holy Spirit to teach me. The Scriptures came alive again. I could not wait to get to my Bible study in the morning because I knew that Jesus, the ultimate rabbi, was teaching me. I gained confidence in depending on the Holy Spirit to guide me into all truth.

In the past, I would sit and listen intently as leaders spoke about their "victories." I became frustrated because I was trying so hard, but did not see that lasting fruit. Instead of receiving what Christ wanted to give me, I had been trying to get it myself by following another person's battle plan. Now I was focused more fully on Jesus, being taught as the Holy Spirit led me ... and I began to see fruit.

Spiritual wholeness does not come through a regimen, but a Redeemer. The Holy Spirit will lead us to spiritual wholeness.

Don't get me wrong—I love and need teaching from my pastor and other Christians. However, they are only part of my spiritual journey. I depend on Christ as my leader.

Stop Following Formulas ... Begin to Follow Jesus

God wants all his children to receive their spiritual inheritance, but he may give each one a different battle plan. We all have different personalities, different hurts, and different backgrounds. Our breakthroughs come when we stop following formulas and follow our Savior. Do not put God in a box. Jesus knows exactly what you need. That is why a personal relationship with Jesus Christ is so important.

If I give you a formula instead of encouraging you to be led by the Spirit, you will fall from grace and go back under the law (Galatians 5:4,18). The laws, the formulas, the religion will never save you. When Joshua was obedient to God and followed the commander of the Lord's army, he saw victory. God gave him a different battle plan each time. What worked in the past may not work in the future. God's plan is always the best plan for the current situation.

Encourage and Help One Another

As we seek to be led by the Spirit, we need the accountability of a body of believers where Christ is the focus. In the battles we will face in our Promised Land, we need a place to regroup and renew our minds with the message of the grace and truth of the Word.

When the battle of Ai was over, Joshua called the men, women, and children together. He built an altar, sacrificed burnt and peace offerings, wrote the law on stones, and read the blessings and cursing as prescribed by Moses (Deuteronomy 27–28). Joshua regrouped with the Israelites to reaffirm their covenant with God.

All the Old Testament sacrifices point to Christ, God's perfect sacrifice. The burnt offering was given on Mount Ebal, the mountain of cursing, and points to the curse of the law being broken through Christ. The peace offering points to our peace with God because of Christ. We became a sweet aroma to the Lord because he sees Jesus in us. Not only did we receive forgiveness, but also the righteousness of Christ.

Joshua's reading and writing of the Old Testament Scriptures points to the truth that sets us free. Jesus is the truth. As you seek to follow Christ, become a part of a body of believers where the gospel is preached without reservation and the Bible is revered as God's truth.

One Name

Jesus. One name above every name. One answer for us all. Christ is the Savior, the Redeemer, and the Healer. We cannot change people's lives, but Christ can. Transformation occurs through him. Christ is the answer for a lost world and for your troubles. He is the way, the truth, and the light.

Bring your hidden hurts into the light through confession and repentance. Then arise and follow Christ. Jesus is the only one who can restore us. Follow him with your whole heart, and watch your life transform.

Key Treasure

Spiritual wholeness does not come through a regimen, but a Redeemer. The Holy Spirit will lead us to spiritual wholeness.

Chapter 7
VICTORY!

My nourish notes for Joshua 9-12

Day 1: Reveal

Meditate on the scriptures, prayerfully reading and reflecting on the verses. Mark the phrases, verses, or words that catch your attention. Journal and learn more as the Lord leads you.

Day 2: Respond

Respond to activate truth in your life. The **IMPACT** acronym provides questions to help you apply the Word. Sometimes you may not have an answer to all six questions.

Image of God to trust? *An attribute of God, Jesus, or the Holy Spirit to trust.*

Message to share? *A word of encouragement, truth, or a prayer to share with others.*

Promise to treasure? *A promise in the Bible to stand on by faith.*

Action to take? *A specific step God is calling you to take.*

Core authentic identity to embrace? *A truth about how God sees you to agree with in your heart.*

Transgression to confess or forgive? *A confession to receive healing, help, and restoration through Christ.*

Day 3: Renew

Carry God's Word with you during the week. Renew your mind daily by focusing on one word, verse, or truth that the Holy Spirit revealed through the Bible. Like an anchor that secures its vessel, renewing your mind with the truth brings security and focus, despite the waves you face during the day.

My Anchor of Truth:

NOURISH JOURNAL

Additional space to record any further thoughts God has shared with me.

DAY 4

God himself put it this way: "I'll live in them, move into them; I'll be their God and they'll be my people. So leave the corruption and compromise; leave it for good," says God. —*2 Corinthians 6:16–17 MSG*

The grand finale of Joshua's conquest of the Promised Land begins in chapter 9. Up until now, Joshua and the Israelites have conquered two cities with three battles. The battle plan picks up momentum until the Israelites, with the full force of their God behind them, first sweep the Amorites, then the southern kingdoms, and finally move to take the northern kingdoms of the Promised Land. There is something wonderful and awesome about seeing God's plan come to completion and watching the Israelites come into their place of rest.

No One Can Stop God's Plan

This scene opens up in chapter 9 with a group of kings from west of the Jordan who were very frightened of the Israelites. All the kingdoms had heard about the defeat of Jericho and Ai. The Amorite kings knew that the God of the Israelites was more powerful than anything they had on their side. Pushing back Jericho, walls falling at the sound of trumpets—the God of Abraham proved to be a force worth fearing. In an effort to save their kingdoms, the Amorite kings banned together.

It is interesting to reflect back on the beginning of Joshua's adventure. Remember how God had to tell him over and over again to be strong and courageous? Now the very enemies that had terrified Joshua were terrified of him! No man can thwart God's plan. No man can shut the doors God opens for us (Revelation 3:8). What a blessing to know that when we are following God, no one can stop his purpose in our lives!

Things Are Not Always as They Appear to Be

The Gibeonites did not band together with the rest of the kingdoms from the west of the Jordan. Instead, they decided to deceive the Israelites into a covenant relationship with them.

God had commanded the Israelites not to leave survivors: "In the cities of the nations the LORD your God is giving you as an inheritance, do not leave alive anything that breathes. Completely destroy them" (Deuteronomy 20:16–17). Apparently, the Gibeonites found out about God's command. Even though they lived only five miles from Jerusalem, they decided to protect themselves by posing as foreigners from outside of Canaan. If they could convince the Israelites that they were not neighboring Canaanites, perhaps they could build a lasting safety net by persuading the Israelites to form a covenant relationship with them.

The Gibeonites wore tattered and patched clothing and brought food that would suggest they had journeyed a long way. Their wineskins were cracked and mended. The bread was dry and moldy. The Gibeonites cleverly offered themselves as Israel's servant in exchange for a peace treaty covenant. It had been over 400 years since anyone had served the Israelites—perhaps they thought that the Gibeonites were actually a blessing from God. They examined the evidence, and everything suggested the Gibeonites were foreigners. Based on the evidence, the Israelites made a covenant with the Gibeonites.

However, the Bible says that the Israelites made this decision without inquiring of the Lord. Sometimes we make decisions based only on what we see with our natural eyes. God wants us to see with our spiritual eyes by abiding in him and looking to him for discernment. Just because something looks good and the circumstances line up, it is not necessarily God's choice for us. Proverbs 14:12 says, "There is a way that appears to be right, but in the end it leads to death." If Joshua had inquired of the Lord, he would have learned that this was not a covenant relationship he needed to form.

Only three days later, Joshua discovered that the Israelites had made a terrible mistake. The Gibeonites were actually their neighbors. Biblical covenants were binding and obligated the Israelites to protect the Gibeonites for the rest of their lives. Because of the binding covenant, the Israelites later rescued the Gibeonites from the attack of neighboring kingdoms. The Israelites could not fulfill God's commandment to destroy all the inhabitants of the Promised Land because they could not destroy the Gibeonites. Not only in Joshua's generation, but also for future generations, the covenant obligation would remain. In fact, many years later Saul brought great judgment on Israel when he decided to attack the Gibeonites. Israel faced famine for three years until David offered restitution (2 Samuel 21:1).

I know that I've made many wrong turns because something looked good on the outside, and I failed to pause and seek God's guidance. It takes a lot of Holy Spirit empowered self-control to stop and inquire of the Lord. Busyness can prevent us from taking the time to seek God—and sometimes we simply want to do things our way. The Bible tells us to "trust in the LORD with all your heart, and lean not on your own understanding; in all your ways acknowledge Him, and He shall direct your paths" (Proverbs 3:5–6 NKJV).

Are you in the middle of making a major decision? If so, stop! Take the time to pull back and inquire of God.

Always Seek God's Guidance in Your Relationships

Proverbs 12:26 says, "The righteous choose their friends carefully, but the way of the wicked leads them astray." It is only when we ask God for discernment that you and I can make good decisions.

God cares very much about the people with whom we come into a covenant-type relationship. Don't get me wrong—God wants us to minister to everyone. Ministry is for everyone, but intimate fellowship is only for a few. The reason God commanded the Israelites to destroy the inhabitants of the Promised Land was to protect them from idolatry. Likewise, for our own protection, God calls us to be cautious about our binding, personal relationships.

At some point in our lives, most of us, like the Israelites, have experienced the devastating effects of a wrong relationship. Maybe as soon as three days after your marriage you realized you had made a mistake. Perhaps you have entered into a business relationship with someone who did not share your values. Could it be that some of your friends encouraged you to sin instead of helping you make right choices? Maybe a close friend you trusted betrayed you, and now you see that you never should have trusted this person in the first place.

If you currently feel trapped in a relationship that does not honor God, know that he can redeem anything. First, do not beat yourself up for making a wrong turn. The enemy does a great job of condemning us, and we do not need to give him any additional help! Just as the Israelites were deceived by the Gibeonites, we too can be a victim of manipulation. If you sense people using deception or manipulation, you can be assured that their actions are not from God. Watch out!

Second, know that God turned the Israelites' trouble into hope by turning the curse of the Gibeonites into a blessing. When Joshua fought for the Gibeonites, he wiped out five key kings at one time! Many years later, the Gibeonites were still the Israelites' servants and eventually helped Nehemiah rebuild the temple. Ultimately, the Israelites were not trapped by entering the wrong relationship—and neither are you. Cry out to God and watch him deliver you.

The Israelites were living in enemy territory, and so they had to be cautious about their relationships. Likewise, believers, this is not our home and we need to be cautious about our close alliances. This is not a call to paranoia—but I am urging you to be wise. Pray for discernment so that your friendships will encourage you by pointing you to Christ, not devour you. Love everyone, but do not compromise when it comes to choosing your close, binding relationships.

Our close personal relationships are not the only issues in our lives that are not up for compromise. What the Gibeonites wore and carried to trick the Israelites symbolizes three other areas that should not be up for negotiation: grace, the authority of God's Word, and our identity in Christ.

Mixing Law with Grace

God does not want us to compromise grace by putting ourselves back under the law. The Gibeonites carried old wineskins. Jesus said, "No one sews a patch of unshrunk cloth on an old garment, for the patch will pull away from the garment, making the tear worse. Neither do people pour new wine into old wineskins. If they do, the skins will burst;

the wine will run out and the wineskins will be ruined. No, they pour new wine into new wineskins, and both are preserved" (Matthew 9:16–17). Putting new wine into old wineskins speaks of mixing the old covenant back into the new.

We cannot mix grace with the law. It is easy for the law to creep back into our lives because it gives us a reason to feel good about ourselves and our ability. Paul confronted Peter and other Jewish Christians for being legalistic about circumcision (Galatians 1–3). We cannot have a religious mindset under the new covenant. Jesus paid a great price so that we could live under grace. He has set us free from the law—let's stay that way.

The Authority of God's Word

God does not want us to compromise the authority of his Word. The Gibeonites brought bread that was dry and moldy. The ways of the world leave us dry and thirsty. Jesus called himself the bread of life. He affirmed that "man shall not live on bread alone, but on every word that comes from the mouth of God" (Matthew 4:4).

We are called to be salt and light to the world. Some relationships encourage us to walk away from the truth and use grace for license to sin. Find friends who sharpen you and encourage you to follow God. Stay close to people who are full of hope in God's promises. Love everyone, but find encouragement from those who point you to Christ. Get to know those who want to be obedient to Christ. Sharing stories of God's faithfulness will inspire you—and them—to follow the promptings of the Holy Spirit.

Our Identity in Christ

God also does not want us to compromise our new identity in Christ. The Gibeonites wore old clothes and old shoes. When you became a Christian, God put a robe of righteousness on you. Colossians 3:10 encourages us to "put on the new self, which is being renewed in knowledge in the image of its Creator." Your identity is not in those old clothes you used to wear. Do not hang around with others who want you to wear your old clothes. Your identity is now in being a child of God. If others pull you back into old habits, perhaps it's time to end those relationships.

The Bible says, "Bad company corrupts good character" (1 Corinthians 15:33). Know your value in Christ, love and serve everyone, but choose your covenant relationships wisely. Surround yourself with those who have a heart's desire to have brave hearts for the Lord. Seek discernment from the Lord by staying close to him in prayer. Ask God to give you spiritual eyes when you make decisions.

Joshua was called to lead the Israelites into the Promised Land, and although the Gibeonites and the kings tried to stand in the way, God's plan prevailed. As you seek and obey his guidance in every area of your life, his plan for you will surely prevail.

Onward!

DAY 5

Those who hope in the LORD will renew their strength. They will soar on wings like eagles; they will run and not grow weary, they will walk and not be faint.
—*Isaiah 40:31*

"Never give up. Never back down. Never lose faith." This is the message from *Facing the Giants*. Written and directed by Alex and Stephen Kendrick in 2006, this movie is about a football team that, against all odds, won the state championship. Through a series of circumstances and an intense time in prayer, the coach renewed his mind and recognized the fact that all things are possible with God. He changed his team motto to challenge his players to always give God their best and leave the results up to him. Although his team had the most difficult schedule and was the smallest team in school history, they played with all of their hearts, faced their giants, and became state champions.[1]

Facing Up to the Giants

Joshua was a mighty warrior because he served God with passion and gave God his best. Although his army was not as big as the Canaanites' and his men were weary, untrained soldiers, Joshua took all the key cities in the southern and northern kingdoms and secured the Israelites' inheritance.

At the end of a seven-year battle, Joshua destroyed the Anakim, the giants living in the Promised Land.[2] Back in the wilderness, when Moses sent twelve spies to the Promised Land, only Joshua and Caleb believed they could overcome the giants. And now we see in the closing battle of Joshua's conquest that Caleb and he had been right. With God on their side, they conquered the giants.

God can overcome any giants. What giants do you see in the world? Hunger … homelessness … suicide? Aids … cancer … autism? What giants do you see in your home? A wayward child … infertility … a broken marriage … a lack of love? What giants do you see within your own life? Anger … unforgiveness … bitterness … fear … anxiety … depression?

God told Joshua he didn't need to be afraid of the giants in his life … and neither do we. Face them. Look to God for your battle plan and your promises. Walk by faith, giving him your absolute best, and he will take care of the rest.

Never give up, never back down, and never ever lose faith. God is so much bigger than any giant you will ever face.

What giants do you dream of conquering?

_____

_____

_____

Rather than face the giants in our world, in our homes, and in us, it is sometimes easier to back down and remain passive. But when we start believing that God is bigger than any giant, we can stop being passive about our walk with him and pursue our calling with relentless passion. Jeremiah 29:11 says, "'For I know the plans I have for you,' declares the LORD, 'plans to prosper you and not to harm you, plans to give you hope and a future.'" However, you will never see those plans come to fruition if you never face up to the giants!

Joshua Was Passionate About God's Plan for His Life

God called Joshua to secure the Promised Land and divide the inheritance among the tribes. Joshua served God with a passion because he knew God's plan for his life.

Jesus wants us to serve him with passion. He said to the church of Laodicea, "I know your deeds, that you are neither cold nor hot. I wish you were either one or the other! So, because you are lukewarm—neither hot nor cold—I am about to spit you out of my mouth" (Revelation 3:15–16). I think it is fascinating that Jesus would rather see us cold for him than lukewarm.

There is absolutely nothing boring about following God. I believe that a lukewarm attitude about serving God comes from having a religious mindset. Filing in and out of a church every week is not all there is to being a Christian. See your life with endless possibilities because you serve the God of the impossible. When you have purpose, you serve God with passion.

Joshua Took Action

Joshua fought with strategy. Biblical scholars suggest that these battles from chapters 9 and 10 occurred over a seven-year period. There are three divisions of battle. First, Joshua defeated the five kings of the Amorites (Joshua 10:1–15). Next, he conquered the southern region by securing Libnah, Lachish, Eglon, Hebron, and Debir (Joshua 10:16–43). Finally, he moved into northern Canaan to secure the entire region of Canaan (Joshua 11). Although there were still smaller cities to be taken, by capturing the key cities, Joshua completed his task and allowed Israel to rest in the Promised Land.

The opposite of passion is being passive. Just because we are led by the Spirit does not mean that we become lazy. God calls us to walk by faith. Walking is an action. Go to God to get your battle plan and then walk by faith, giving God your best and leaving the rest to him.

Joshua Acted on God's Promises

Joshua served God with passion because he acted on the promises of God. The Lord said to Joshua, "Do not be afraid of them; I have given them into your hand. Not one of them will be able to withstand you" (Joshua 10:8; see also Joshua 11:6). God promised Joshua that the land of Canaan was for the Israelites and that every enemy would be defeated.

God promises us that we are the righteousness of God in Christ Jesus. God promises us that we became new creations in Christ. God promises us that sin has lost its control over us.

Joshua could see his enemies and the land that was yet to be taken, but he pursued them with passion because he rested on the promises of God. We may have a hard time believing in our spiritual inheritance because we can still see the giants in our lives. But God wants us to act on the promises that were given to us through the cross.

Joshua had a *brave heart*. He believed God's promises and wholly followed him and utterly destroyed the enemy (Joshua 4:8, 11:9). There are thousands of promises to God's children in the Bible. We can serve God with a passion by believing the promises of God for ourselves. Not only that, but we can share God's faithfulness with others through our testimony. With the five kings of the Amorites defeated, Joshua was finally able to speak the words of encouragement to the Israelites that God had spoken to him back in the wilderness. As the Israelites stood with their feet on the necks of the defeated kings, Joshua told them, "Do not be afraid; do not be discouraged. Be strong and courageous. This is what the Lord will do to all the enemies you are going to fight" (Joshua 10:25).

Just as Joshua passed on his promises from God to the Israelites, we can pass on God's promises to our children. Share stories of God's love and faithfulness with your children. Tell them specifically how you have seen him move in your life. Share answers to prayers. Talk about how he speaks to you through his Word. Teach them to recognize God's miracles in everyday living. Teach them to look for his splendor in creation. When they grow up and face giants of their own, they will remember that the hand of God is mighty.

Joshua Prayed Boldly

Joshua served God with passion because he was not reluctant to pray boldly. When Joshua fought the five kings of the Amorites, he needed a little extra time in his day, so he prayed that the sun would stand still. (I am sure you feel that way every now and then.)

Now, that was a bold prayer! Back in biblical times, people believed that the sun revolved around the earth. Joshua was asking God to make time stand still! The God we serve created the world in six days. For heaven's sake, pray big and bold. Ask for the impossible!

How blessed are we to have the King of all creation listening and answering our prayers. Jesus said, "Ask and it will be given to you" (Matthew 7:7). We serve a big God who not only made the sun stand still but can move mountains in our lives. Child of God, pour your heart out to him and ask for the impossible. *Brave heart*, prayer keeps you dependent on God. When was the last time you poured your heart out to him in your prayer time and asked for the impossible?

Pray boldly and see God answer mightily. Jesus said, "Suppose you have a friend, and you go to him at midnight and say, 'Friend, lend me three loaves of bread; a friend of mine on a journey has come to me, and I have no food to offer him.' And suppose the one inside answers, 'Don't bother me. The door is already locked, and my children and I are in bed. I can't get up and give you anything.' I tell you, even though he will not get up and give you the bread because of friendship, yet because of your **shameless audacity** he will surely get up and give you as much as you need. So I say to you: Ask and it will be given to you; seek and you will find; knock and the door will be opened to you. For everyone who asks receives; the one who seeks finds; and to the one who knocks, the door will be opened (Luke 11:5–10, *emphasis mine*).

Joshua's prayer was not a long one—or even well thought out. It was not a religious prayer, but it was a bold one—and God answered. Because of God's grace, we can expect God to move mountains for us in his own timing according to his will.

A religious mindset might lead you to think you have to earn God's answer or even do your own mountain moving, but faith says stop striving and believe! When we pray boldly, we need to be at peace with the fact that God may tell us "no," and continue to trust him and walk by faith.

Prayer is one of the most powerful actions we can take. It is a part of the armor of God. We can pray anywhere and anytime. What a gift to be able to talk to the Almighty God anytime and lay our worries at his feet. Then we can trust that the God who loves us and is for us will answer our prayers according to his perfect plan.

God is faithful. Have you placed your trust in him?

Joshua Depended on God's Power

Joshua served God with passion because he depended on God's power. I have heard it said that God calls us to do our best with what is possible, and then we can rest in his power, trusting in him to do the impossible.

Joshua and his men marched all night long to attack the Amorites. They gave their best, but I am sure that the all-night walking left them weary. However, God threw the Amorites into confusion and they fled. Finally, the Lord threw hailstones at the Amorites. Miraculously, not one of the stones landed on an Israelite, but all of them landed on the enemy. The battle was won by the power of God.

When Joshua fought the northern kingdom, the historian Josephus tells us that this enemy's coalition numbered 300,000 infantrymen, 10,000 cavalrymen, and 20,000 chariots.[3] This massive army would seem impossible for the Israelites to fight. However, Joshua did as God commanded. He did the possible and allowed God to take care of the impossible. "Surely the LORD was fighting for Israel!" (Joshua 10:14). He is also fighting for you!

Paul prayed that the Ephesians would know they had the resurrection power on the inside of them (Ephesians 1:19–20). Ask God to reveal his plan for your life. Then stand on his promises and rest in his power. Don't just talk about being a Christian—be one! God has a part for you to play in his grand plan. Serve him with passion.

What is impossible in your life when God is on your side? Nothing! When you serve God and resolve to give him the glory, there is no giant He cannot defeat and no door God cannot open. Joshua served the Lord with passion and purpose. Open your eyes wide to the greatness of your God, take a deep breath, and serve him with all your heart.

Key Treasure

Open your eyes wide to the greatness of your God, take a deep breath, and serve him with all your heart.

DAY 6

If Joshua had given them rest, God would not have spoken later about another day. There remains, then, a Sabbath-rest for the people of God; for anyone who enters God's rest also rests from their works, just as God did from his. Let us, therefore, make every effort to enter that rest, so that no one will perish by following their example of disobedience. —*Hebrews 4:8–11*

Without a doubt, besides Christmas and their birthdays, my boys' favorite day of the year is the last day of school. In fact, recently they were actually dancing around the kitchen because the last day of school was approaching. With great excitement, they shouted, "No more school! No more homework! No more work!"

Josh and Justin were pumped that the work was over. They were looking forward to those lazy days of resting over the summer. (Oh, if I could only go back in time …) Even as an adult, when I know a vacation is coming, I am excited as I anticipate rest and relaxation!

Rest from the Battle

After Joshua and his mighty men of valor secured the cities in Canaan, the Bible tells us that the land had rest from war (Joshua 11:23). I can only imagine how the Israelites felt as they found themselves finally at a place of security and rest. Their history for the previous 447 years had been anything but rest. The Israelites had been slaves in Egypt for four hundred years. After God delivered them from slavery, they spent forty years in the wilderness. Even after they crossed the Jordan into the Promised Land, they spent some seven more years pursuing their enemies to possess their inheritance. I wonder if they ever thought, *Are we ever going to get to our place of rest?*

Now that the battles were over, they could finally rest. They saw God's faithfulness to his promise of Canaan he had made to Father Abraham so many years before. The land flowing with milk and honey was finally theirs to enjoy. The land was at rest, and the Israelites were home.

The word *rest* in that scripture is the Hebrew word *shaquat*, which means to be quiet, tranquil, and at peace.[4] There are all kinds of wars going on today: wars on our health, wars on the family, war within our country, wars between countries. The world is looking everywhere for peace. However, lasting rest only comes through our Redeemer, Jesus. No amount of government can build it, no amount of money can buy it, and no doctor can prescribe a pill for the peace and rest that come through Christ's love for us.

As we have said before, Joshua is a picture of the pre-incarnate Christ. Hebrews 4:8 tells us that Joshua brought the Israelites into their rest. However, there is also rest for every child of God from the war within our souls. Just as Joshua was the one God had chosen to take the Israelites into the Promised Land, Jesus Christ is the only one who can give us eternal rest.

Believe in the Goodness and Love of God

The Israelites were delivered from their bondage in Egypt but never entered the Promised Land. Similarly, you can trust Christ for your salvation, and yet never enter into a place of rest because of your unbelief in the goodness of God. "Out of his fullness we have all received grace in place of grace already given. For the law was given through Moses; grace and truth came through Jesus Christ" (John 1:16–17).

> Read Hebrews 3:16–4:10 aloud. Why were the Israelites unable to enter the Promised Land? Is your walk with God one of peace and rest? Why or why not?

The Israelites were not able to enter into the Promised Land because of unbelief. Do you believe in the goodness of God? Are you certain that he is on your side and will never forsake you?

Only Joshua and Caleb had faith in God's promise about the land of Canaan (Numbers 14). From that generation of Israelites, only Joshua and Caleb were able to enter the Promised Land. In the wilderness, the Israelites were guilty of idolatry, immorality, and grumbling … but it was their unbelief in God's goodness that kept them out of the Promised Land.

The gospel is never about what we do. It is not about us and how we will keep the Ten Commandments. The gospel of Jesus Christ is about what he has done for us.

Unbelief will keep you out of the land flowing with milk and honey. Instead of believing that God is not happy with you because perhaps you did not have your quiet time today or go to church last Sunday, start resting in his unconditional love. Don't allow your heart to get in the way of his.

Stop trying to earn his favor! God blesses us with every spiritual blessing in Christ—not because of what we do but because of who we are in Christ. On the cross Jesus said, "It is finished" (John 19:30). The work is complete. God loves us and wants to bless us. Now it is up to us to believe.

Keep in Step with the Holy Spirit

Our rest in Christ opens up a new way of living and resting: following the Holy Spirit. If we live in bondage to sin, we are not really at rest (2 Peter 2:19; John 8:33–35; Romans 6:16–23). Jesus died so that we could live for God (Galatians 2:20). He has given us a new way to live—by the power of the Holy Spirit!

When we accept God's free gift of salvation by receiving Jesus as our Savior from sin and making him Lord of our lives, we are instantly clothed in the righteousness of Christ (Philippians 3:9). God looks at us and sees us cleansed, white as snow (Isaiah 1:18). But now it is time for the walk, the process of growing and becoming more like Jesus in our words and actions. This is a lifelong process: a struggle between walking in the flesh and the Spirit. Resting in versus resisting the Holy Spirit.

Listen ... and Follow

Rest comes when we stop trying to control our lives and start living for God. God's principles bring peace to our souls. As we listen and follow Jesus, he transforms us inwardly so that we can live for God with *brave hearts*.

Becoming a *brave heart* is not about following religious rules, but listening to the voice of our Redeemer and following it. Jesus said, "Why do you call me, 'Lord, Lord,' and do not do what I say? As for everyone who comes to me and hears my words and puts them into practice, I will show you what they are like. They are like a man building a house, who dug down deep and laid the foundation on rock. When a flood came, the torrent struck that house but could not shake it, because it was well built" (Luke 6:46–48).

Listen! "If you hear his voice, do not harden your hearts" (Hebrews 3:7–8). God built the earth with his wisdom (Proverbs 3:19). God has given us his Word and his Spirit to empower us to walk with a *brave heart* and follow kingdom principles.

When we are at rest, the Word no longer condemns us—it sanctifies us! (John 17:17). After we get our arms around God's love for us, we can rest as we read the Word because our fear of punishment is gone. "The word of God is alive and active. Sharper than any double-edged sword, it penetrates even to dividing soul and spirit, joints and marrow; it judges the thoughts and attitudes of the heart" (Hebrews 4:12). Read your Bible not to get God's love but to find out about his love for you. We learn more and more about the blessings of God through the Word. We learn more about God's character through the Word. We learn more about the thousands of promises that are ours through the Word. Allow the Word to transform you under the canopy of his grace! The truth will set you free.

You are in Christ. Rest. When you expect God's goodness, you will see his love for you everywhere. Joshua rescued the Israelites from the wilderness and led them into the Promised Land. Jesus rescues us from the old covenant to the new. Rest in the power of the cross. Rest in the power of the Holy Spirit to live for God. Rest in his ways and live in expectancy of God's blessings in your life. Drink in God's love for you.

Rest in Serving Others

Not only can we rest as we sow into God's principles to position ourselves for blessing, but we can also find rest in humbling ourselves by becoming servants to others. When we get close to the things God's heart beats for there is rest.

Christ chose to leave heaven, come to earth, and humble himself on the cross so that you and I could have eternal life. He could have taken care of his enemies with one blow, but he chose to walk in love. He could have taken the kingdom, but he chose to walk out God's will for his life. He could have walked away from the beatings, the ridicule, and the pain of nails in his hands, but he chose anguish so that we could have eternal life. Oh yes, Jesus could have done anything he wanted. He is God. But he chose to serve, to endure the cross, so that we could have eternal life.

I have spent much of my life trying to learn about what is mine through Christ. That is not a bad thing. However, I am beginning to see that I will never be at rest until I stop looking to Christ for what I can get and start looking to Christ to empower me to *give*.

We may have to pass by earthly rewards, but our reward in heaven is far greater. While you have this short time on earth, will you live in view of eternal rewards? Jesus did.

> In humility value others above yourselves, not looking to your own interests but each of you to the interests of the others. In your relationships with one another, have the same mindset as Christ Jesus: Who, being in very nature God, did not consider equality with God something to be used to his own advantage; rather, he made himself nothing by taking the very nature of a servant, being made in human likeness. And being found in appearance as a man, he humbled himself by becoming obedient to death— even death on a cross! Therefore God exalted him to the highest place and gave him the name that is above every name, that at the name of Jesus every knee should bow, in heaven and on earth and under the earth, and every tongue acknowledge that Jesus Christ is Lord, to the glory of God the Father. (Philippians 2:3–11)

We may not receive our reward this side of heaven, but things like money, titles, material items, and status will one day fade away. The prophets and the patriarchs never saw the Messiah in their lifetime, yet they continued to believe in the goodness of God and live for him. We can rest in the fact that we will one day live in our eternal home and lay our crowns at his feet.

Revelation 12:11 says, "They triumphed over him by the blood of the Lamb and by the word of their testimony; they did not love their lives so much as to shrink from death."

Do you want to be an overcomer? There is rest, child of God, in your position in Christ through the blood of the Lamb … in kingdom principles in the Word of *his* testimony … and in the passion of loving others as we die to self.

Be Still ... and Know That I Am God

I just started subscribing to a daily email devotion from Living Free ministries (www.LivingFree.org). This particular devotion seems to be the perfect ending to today's reading. I hope you enjoy reading it as much as I did. Rest and be blessed!

Be still ...

Stop worrying. Calm down. Don't be afraid. Stop trying to figure it out by yourself. Stop trying to make things happen. Slow down. Take a deep breath. Forget the money crunch. Take time out from the pressures at work. Stop striving. Stop talking ... and listen.

Know that I am God ...

I know you. I know your needs. Nothing surprises me. I am the Creator of all things. I care about everything that concerns you. I am love. I am peace. I am joy. I am holy. I am sovereign. I am all-knowing. I am all-powerful. I am eternal. I am faithful. I am merciful. I am gracious. I am the King of kings and Lord of lords. I am your Father, your Daddy. I am the same yesterday, today and forever. I love you with an everlasting love. I will never leave you nor forsake you.

Consider this ...

When we are willing to be still ... and to know that he is God, he will become the center of our lives. And everything else we do will revolve around him and all that he is.[5]

Key Treasure

You are in Christ. Rest. When you expect God's goodness, you will see his love for you everywhere.

Chapter 8

YOUR CALL, YOUR CHOICE

My nourish notes for Joshua 13-21

Day 1: Reveal

Meditate on the scriptures, prayerfully reading and reflecting on the verses. Mark the phrases, verses, or words that catch your attention. Journal and learn more as the Lord leads you.

Day 2: Respond

Respond to activate truth in your life. The **IMPACT** acronym provides questions to help you apply the Word. Sometimes you may not have an answer to all six questions.

Image of God to trust? *An attribute of God, Jesus, or the Holy Spirit to trust.*

Message to share? *A word of encouragement, truth, or a prayer to share with others.*

Promise to treasure? *A promise in the Bible to stand on by faith.*

Action to take? *A specific step God is calling you to take.*

Core authentic identity to embrace? *A truth about how God sees you to agree with in your heart.*

Transgression to confess or forgive? *A confession to receive healing, help, and restoration through Christ.*

Day 3: Renew

Carry God's Word with you during the week. Renew your mind daily by focusing on one word, verse, or truth that the Holy Spirit revealed through the Bible. Like an anchor that secures its vessel, renewing your mind with the truth brings security and focus, despite the waves you face during the day.

My Anchor of Truth:

NOURISH JOURNAL

Additional space to record any further thoughts God has shared with me.

DAY 4

For we are God's handiwork, created in Christ Jesus
to do good works, which God prepared in advance for us to do.
—*Ephesians 2:10*

Did you know that you are a divine creation? The Bible says that we are fearfully and wonderfully made (Psalm 139:14). You were designed by God, and when he designed you, he was not using a formula. He was flowing with the creativity of his divine nature. He gave you your strengths and your weaknesses. He put likes and dislikes in you. He gave you dreams. He made a masterpiece when he made you. You are "a kind of firstfruit" among his creations (James 1:18). He didn't overlook any detail. He even knows the number of hairs on your head (Luke 12:7). You are a designer's original.

God was not concerned with worldly standards when he made you. He did not use a mold or cookie cutter. He did not copy you from a magazine cover. He was not concerned with lining you up for perfection. He chose to create you and design you so that you could fulfill your purpose in life.

God Has a Plan for Your Life—
a Unique and Special Purpose

The Lord gave each of us particular gifts according to his plan for us (1 Corinthians 12:4–12). We are anointed to carry out different callings. When we find our purpose, we are to use our gifts to accomplish God's plan for us instead of putting ourselves into someone else's mold, trying to be someone we were not designed to be, desiring someone else's gifts. Only then are we free to follow the Holy Spirit in fulfilling our calling.

Joshua had two jobs: to bring the Israelites into the Promised Land and to give each tribe of Israel its allotment (Joshua 11:23). Jesus is the only one who can bring you into your Promised Land, and Jesus is the only one who can show you your place there. All Israelites were God's chosen people, but they lived in different tribes, with different borders. As Christians, we are all God's children, but we have different allotments and different boundaries—gifts and callings—that Jesus gives us through the Holy Spirit. True freedom comes when we follow Jesus to become the women and men God created us to be.

Just as God defined the physical land boundaries for the Israelites, God defines the boundaries of our Promised Land: who we are, what gifts we have, and how we are to use those gifts. True success is not measured by the world or other people. True success is defined as knowing God's will and doing it.

Jeremiah 29:11 says, "'I know the plans I have for you,' declares the LORD, 'plans to prosper you and not to harm you, plans to give you hope and a future.'" In this scripture, God says, "I know." In other words, it is the Lord who knows the most marvelous plan for our lives. Even though God has designed us for his purpose and has plans to prosper us, I am afraid many of us do not know what those plans are because we have not allowed the Lord to define them for us.

I encourage you to listen to God. Your parents, your friends, or a counselor might be able to give you wise counsel based on what they have experienced and learned, but they cannot give you your allotment in the Promised Land. Jesus is the only one who can define your borders. Allow him to be your life coach!

God Gives Perfect Boundaries

The Israelites were divided into twelve tribes. Those tribes stemmed from the twelve sons of Jacob, Abraham's grandson. Because the twelve sons of Jacob—Reuben, Simeon, Levi, Judah, Issachar, Zebulon, Gad, Asher, Dan, Naphtali, Joseph, and Benjamin—were Abraham's great-grandchildren, they were part of the Israelite nation (Genesis 46:8–25, 49:1–28). The descendents of each of Jacob's twelve sons represent those tribes. The tribe of Joseph is composed of two half tribes descending from Joseph's sons, Manasseh and Ephraim.

The Levites made up the "priestly tribe." They were ordained by God to carry out the many duties required to keep the tabernacle running smoothly. God did not give them a large land inheritance all in one area. Instead, he scattered them throughout Canaan and placed them in cities with pasturelands (Joshua 21:8). In his wisdom, God did this so his Word would be scattered throughout the Promised Land. God did not give the Levites big parcels of land to take care of. As priests, they were busy and had many responsibilities. Bigger boundaries would have been a burden. God sets perfect boundaries.

The psalmist says, "The boundary lines have fallen for me in pleasant places; surely I have a delightful inheritance" (Psalm 16:6). God gives us all different gifts and callings. The boundaries we have are perfect—anything more would be a burden. He has created us and knows what is best for us. Looking beyond your borders prevents you from cultivating *your* God-given gifts.

> How does 1 Corinthians 12:7–26 encourage you to celebrate your own boundaries or spiritual gifts from the Holy Spirit?

Seek Jesus with Boldness to Find Your Life's Purpose

The tribes of Judah and Ephraim and the half tribe of Manasseh were the forward-thinking tribes because they sought out Joshua for their allotment (Joshua 14–17). The tribe of Judah settled in the south of Canaan (Joshua 15). Joseph's descendents, the half tribes of Manasseh and Ephraim, were allotted the hill country in the north. They were so bold and confident that they asked Joshua to expand their borders (Joshua 17:14–17).

Seek Jesus with the boldness of Caleb and Joseph's descendants to find your life's purpose. Own your calling—it is a gift from the Lord. Don't be insecure or timid—that is not true humility. "I remind you to fan into flame the gift of God, which is in you through the laying on of my hands. For the Spirit God gave us does not make us timid, but gives us power, love, and self-discipline" (2 Timothy 1:6–7).

Jesus did not die to give us the Promised Land so we could go our own way, doing our own thing. Take hold of the calling in your life by pressing into Jesus and following the voice of the Holy Spirit. Be willing to be all God created you to be, *brave heart*!

Dreams Are Personal and Unique …
Rejoice in Yours and Encourage Others in Theirs

Be careful that in your excitement about your own dreams, you do not try to force your dreams on other people—especially your children. We may have the best intentions for our children, but we make a mistake if we try to force them into a calling that is not their own. Discipline your children, disciple them—but don't ever touch their dreams (Ephesians 6:4). That is God's area alone. He has given them gifts, and he has a unique plan and purpose for each of them. Children will naturally want to please their parents and might be willing to leave their own dream to join you in yours. Are you willing to let your children go by giving them the freedom to be who God created them to be? What can you do to encourage them to find their own place in the Promised Land?

Parents are responsible for leading and guiding their children, but only Jesus gives them their calling. Get behind their dreams but don't try to manipulate them. When you try to force your agendas on your children, you are playing God—and that is dangerous territory!

Just as you shouldn't force your Promised Land allotment on someone else, neither should you want to enter another person's borders in the Promised Land. God loves you the way you are. He designed you to accomplish your special calling. We miss the joy and freedom of becoming all that God has designed us to be when we try to be like someone else. Jesus can remove the layers of voices and circumstances that are keeping you from being who he created you to be. Stop trying to fit into someone else's allotment. You will never be happy there.

Allow Jesus to Set Your Boundaries

Freedom comes when we have enough courage to follow the Holy Spirit and allow Jesus to define the boundaries of our Promised Land: who we are, what gifts we have, and how we are to use those gifts. The Holy Spirit will reveal God's marvelous plan for our lives if we pursue Jesus. "'What no eye has seen, what no ear has heard, and what no human mind has conceived'—the things God has prepared for those who love him—these are the things God has revealed to us by his Spirit" (1 Corinthians 2:9–10). Stop allowing the world to set your standards for excellence, and look to Jesus for your boundaries. Value and believe in the divine creation that you are. God does not make mistakes. You are perfectly designed to do what he has called you to do. A divine creation!

It does not matter how old you are. As long as you are still drawing breath, it is never too late. Caleb, from the tribe of Judah, did not allow his old age to get in the way of serving the Lord (Joshua 14:10–12). The Lord told Joshua when he had grown old that there was land yet to be taken (Joshua 13:1). Perhaps you thought it was too late to live out those desires God has put in your heart. Think again. Today is always a great day to begin your adventure with Jesus—whether you are twenty-five or ninety-five.

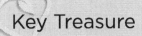

Key Treasure

Jesus can remove the layers of voices and circumstances that are keeping you from being who he created you to be. Stop trying to fit into someone else's allotment. You will never be happy there.

DAY 5

My companions who went with me discouraged the people, but I stuck to my guns, totally with GOD, my God. —*Joshua 14:8 MSG*

Whatever you do, work at it with all your heart, as working for the Lord, not for human masters, since you know that you will receive an inheritance from the Lord as a reward. It is the Lord Christ you are serving. —*Colossians 3:23–24*

If you want to be effective in your Promised Land calling, you need to focus. Make no mistake—as we seek to be *brave hearts*, distractions will come our way. You and I must determine to serve the Lord with our whole heart (Matthew 22:37). Jesus gave his life so we could live in the Promised Land. Such an extreme sacrifice deserves an extreme commitment. The reality is, when we survey the cross, our response could only be a radical one—following the Lord with our whole heart (Romans 12:1–2).

The Bible says that Caleb, Joshua's sidekick, followed the Lord "wholeheartedly" (Joshua 14:8,14). The word *wholeheartedly* is the Hebrew word *male*, which means to be full, satisfied, and complete.[1] Imagine a cup that is filled to the brim with water—it has no more room for anything else. Caleb was full of the Lord's calling in his life—there was no room for any distractions.

Stay Focused on Jesus and His Purpose for Your Life

In his first letter to the Corinthians, Paul explained that he did not run aimlessly—he focused on getting the prize (1 Corinthians 9:22–26). I have been guilty of running fast but without focus. I have been active but aimless. My cup was filled with commitments, but I was not effective in fulfilling my calling because my calendar was filled with distractions. Jesus said, "Take my yoke upon you and learn from me, for I am gentle and humble in heart, and you will find rest for your souls. For my yoke is easy and my burden is light" (Matthew 11:29–30). If we are taking on yokes that are not ours, we lose our focus and become worn-out—and distracted.

Today we are going to look at Joshua's sidekick Caleb to learn how we can remain focused in our callings. God does not want us to live in a flustered, ambivalent state—he wants us to stay focused on our purpose, making every minute count. Time is valuable. Once spent it is gone forever.

In Joshua chapter 14, Caleb, a member of the tribe of Judah, approached Joshua at Gilgal to receive his promised piece of Canaan. "I was forty years old when Moses the servant of the LORD sent me from Kadesh Barnea to explore the land. And I brought him back a report according to my convictions, but my fellow Israelites who went up with me made the hearts of the people melt with fear. I, however, followed the LORD my God wholeheartedly. So on that day Moses swore to me, 'The land on which your feet have walked will be your inheritance and that of your children forever, because you have followed the LORD my God wholeheartedly'" (Joshua 14:7–9).

Because of his conviction to follow the Lord wholeheartedly, Caleb was free to be a trail-blazer, even though that meant going against popular opinion. Many times God will call us to be a trailblazer by being the "first" at something. That can mean going against popular opinion to get the job done. If we are seeking man's approval, we will find it impossible to serve Christ. However, if we are seeking only God's approval, we will be set free to step out boldly into unchartered territory (Galatians 1:10).

Caleb was free from the distraction of needing the approval of his fellow Israelites. He was the first to speak up and state with conviction that he was fully persuaded that God could bring them into their Promised Land. We can all follow God when there is a crowd cheering us on. Stepping out alone on our convictions takes courage.

When we are focused on people's favor, we will be distracted from our destiny. I have struggled with needing the approval of others and was easily distracted and worn-out from trying to make others happy. My motives for serving others were not pure. I was driven by guilt, the need to be well liked by others, and a desire for accolades from man. I was doing many good deeds, but they were flesh driven instead of spirit driven. Because I started these deeds in the flesh, I had to continue in the flesh to try to make them succeed— leaving me frustrated and worn-out (John 3:6).

When our Holy Spirit convictions—instead of our need to have approval—lead us, we will be a focused force. God is the one who gives us favor with man (Psalm 5:12; Proverbs 3:4). Following the crowd for the sake of being liked by everyone will distract us. The need for people's approval does not have to control our decisions (1 Corinthians 4:1–4). When we are filled with the knowledge that favor comes from God, we are free to follow the leading of the Holy Spirit to accomplish what he has called us to do.

Jesus was radical because he sought to do only God's will. God has given believers the authority in Jesus' name and the empowerment of the Holy Spirit to accomplish his purpose for our journey—even when he leads us on roads less traveled.

My grandmother, who is my namesake, loved the Lord, loved her family, and loved playing her violin. Music was a God-given talent that she shared with the community as first string in her city's symphony. Even though she was a master at violin and could make those strings sing and dance, she had to be courageous when the Lord called her to share her gift in the church. She could perform with beautiful precision but had to be brave to bear the disapproval of some church members. It is hard to imagine in our day of contemporary worship that the sweet sound of a first-string violin could offend people. But in my grandmother's day, there were those in the congregation who raised their eyebrows when a young woman led worship by playing her violin.

My grandmother was a *brave heart*—not in a loud and rebellious way. She was a quiet, surrendered woman who simply sought to serve her Savior. She was content to do his will for her life, even when others did not believe in what she was doing.

Jesus was not only her Savior—he was her Lord. I believe the day she first played in the church, it was for an audience of one—Jesus. I have her Bible, and in the front cover she has written these words:

> **The basic factor in becoming a Christian is a personal commitment to Jesus Christ as Savior, Lord, and Master. The Christian life is the obedient fulfillment of the commitment.**

She was a trailblazer, and in her wake, she paved the way for the unbelievable music program that still exists inside her church today. When we are no longer distracted by the need to be liked by everyone, we are free to follow the Lord wholeheartedly. Because Caleb was not distracted by the doubting Israelites, he pressed on into the Promised Land. I believe his *brave heart* inspired Joshua to be strong and courageous.

Patience Helps Us Stay Focused

Caleb waited forty-five years to see the blessings come from his wholehearted obedience. The wait was filled with wandering in the wilderness and wartime in the Promised Land, but he remained patient—and focused. It is easy to become frustrated when we don't see God come through according to our schedule. Impatience can be a huge distraction because we may give up, lose faith, and never see the blessings from obedience. God's calendar is usually different from ours! A friend just told me that her pastor says one of God's characteristics is that he is SLOW—but, of course, he is always right on time. How true! What promise of God have you not yet seen become a reality? What dream is still just a dream? What prayer request is waiting to be answered? Don't allow impatience to distract and dilute your faith!

> Read James 5:7–11. How does patience keep us focused? How can impatience distract us from our callings?

If I were to plant a seed in my backyard and become frustrated after two weeks because I could not see any fruit, I might give up and stop watering the plant, causing it to die. Imagine the prophets in the Old Testament who never saw the Messiah, yet continued by faith to believe, wait, and stand firm in their convictions. As we follow God, we must keep our faith during the wait to receive the blessing of the harvest. Studying God's Word, giving, praying, fasting, walking in love, allowing God to be our defender, meditating, and praying for a lost family member are examples of seeds we sow. Impatience says, "This is not working!" and gives up. Patience says, "I will wait upon the Lord and remain steadfast."

Obedience to the leading of the Holy Spirit always brings blessing. Delays of the harvest can often distract us from a diligent attitude in following God. The book of Galatians says this so well: "A man reaps what he sows. Whoever sows to please their flesh, from the flesh will reap destruction; whoever sows to please the Spirit, from the Spirit will reap eternal life. Let us not become weary in doing good, for at the proper time we will reap a harvest if we do not give up" (Galatians 6:7–9).

If God has given you a dream—don't give up. Be patient and continue to water it with your faith in the Word of God. If God has laid on your heart a family member to pray for— don't give up! If God has given you promises of healing, restoration, or reconciliation— don't ever give up. If you continue to sow seed into another person's life and you don't see results—don't give up!

During the wait, be diligent. Caleb did not grumble but fought right alongside Joshua. Caleb kept his focus during those forty years in the wilderness. He did not need any atta-boys or credit—he was content to work behind the scenes. If waiting makes you restless or you do not feel valued unless you are doing something, you may be tempted to move out on your own, not trusting God's plan. Don't go ahead of God—it is wasted energy and a definite distraction. During the wait, God may be preparing you for the next step in your journey. The wait can be a time of prayer and abiding rest. Be patient and persistent and you will see God's blessings in your life. Forty days, forty weeks, or forty years—however long it takes—don't let your impatience deter you from your destiny. Stay focused and follow God wholeheartedly!

Receive ... So That You Can Give

Caleb was not reluctant to receive the harvest of God's blessings in his life because he lived in expectancy of God's blessings and the fulfillment of his promises (Joshua 14:12). Devaluing ourselves can become a distraction because we are not taking hold of all that Christ has given us so we can give out to others. Jesus told his disciples as he sent them out into ministry, "Freely you have received; freely give" (Matthew 10:8).

You cannot give out what you have not recieved. God "comforts us in all our troubles, so that we can comfort those in any trouble with the comfort we ourselves receive from God" (2 Corinthians 1:4). In his New Testament Commentary, Jon Courson states, "This is such a clear passage because it clearly explains to us that the degree we can comfort others is the degree we have been comforted ourselves."[2] If you don't receive God's comfort, you cannot fully comfort others. If you feel guilty about taking times of rest, you will not have the energy to refresh others (Matthew 11:28–30; Luke 10:38–42).

If God has blessed you in any way, are you reluctant to receive the blessing? Let's honor the Lord by receiving what he wants to give us. False humility is selfish because it draws attention to us instead of the Lord (Matthew 6; Colossians 2:20–23). When we refuse God's blessings in our lives in order to be "religious," the result is resentment (Luke 10:40–41). When we are reluctant to receive God's blessings, we will be reluctant to give them out. If we don't receive God's mercy, we cannot be merciful. If we are stingy with ourselves, we will be stingy with others. If God has given us a treasure and we bury it instead of using it for his glory, we are displeasing him and showing great disrespect (Matthew 25:14–30).

Paul goes on to say, "Just as we share abundantly in the sufferings of Christ, so also our comfort abounds through Christ" (2 Corinthians 1:5). I am not suggesting that our lives will be trouble free. No question, there are times of sacrifice, and suffering (2 Corinthians 6:4–10). Indeed, Caleb went through persecution, trials, and warfare. But when it was his time to receive a blessing, he not only received it—he was bold about asking for it! There will always be mountains to climb as you serve the Lord, but when God bestows a blessing in your life, receive it so you will be refreshed and empowered to give to others (Proverbs 11:25).

Jesus gives abundantly—but not in a worldly way. Not as the world gives, but better than the world gives! (John 10:10, 14:27) He blesses us to be a channel of blessing to others.

"God can pour on the blessings in astonishing ways so that you're ready for anything and everything, more than just ready to do what needs to be done. As one psalmist puts it, 'He throws caution to the winds, giving to the needy in reckless abandon. His right-living, right-giving ways never run out, never wear out.' This most generous God who gives seed to the farmer that becomes bread for your meals is more than extravagant with you. He gives you something you can then give away, which grows into full-formed lives, robust in God, wealthy in every way, so that you can be generous in every way, producing with us great praise to God" (2 Corinthians 9:8–11 MSG).

One caution: Being open to receive God's gifts is not a license for greed! Greed will prevent you from giving to others. When greed is in play, you are focused on the gift instead of the giver. When greed is involved, you are wrapped up in how you can take things—God wants you to receive! When we allow God to give to us, his gift is perfect in every way. We think we know what we want, but if we operate out of greed, our eyes are not on Jesus. In that case, when we receive things, they don't truly bless us! They just increase our appetite for more. I am not suggesting materialism—I am encouraging you to live in expectancy of his blessings, knowing that God gives us perfect gifts at the perfect time to equip and motivate us to give to others (Proverbs 22:9,16).

Family First

Obviously Caleb's family was a priority in his life. He was eighty-five and made sure his daughter was secure in a marriage to a man who was not afraid to persevere in battle (Joshua 15:16). He was responsive not only to her needs but was happy to give her the upper and lower springs just as the Lord had so graciously given to him (Joshua 15:19).

Once a reporter asked Mother Teresa how to promote world peace. She responded, "What can you do to promote world peace? Go home and love your family."[3]

As parents, we model God's love to our children. As husbands and wives, we have the opportunity to love our spouses unconditionally. Our callings, if we are not careful, can distract us from our roles as parents and spouses.

I believe there is an anointing that comes when our families become our next priority after our relationship with the Lord (Psalm 133). Because we know our families will always be there for us, we could be tempted to consider time with them less important than work the Lord has given us to do. So many children and spouses are left without love in the name of work or ministry, and it is wrong! Stay focused on Jesus and have right priorities—then God will anoint the work in your hands.

Putting It All Together

Caleb's focus to serve the Lord wholeheartedly is evident as he describes the time in the wilderness:

> My companions who went with me discouraged the people, but I stuck to my guns, totally with GOD, my God. That was the day that Moses solemnly promised, "The land on which your feet have walked will be your inheritance, you and your children's, forever. Yes, you have lived totally for GOD." Now look at me: GOD has kept me alive, as he promised. It is now forty-five years since GOD spoke this word to Moses, years in which Israel wandered in the wilderness. And here I am today, eighty-five years old! I'm as strong as I was the day Moses sent me out. I'm as strong as ever in battle, whether coming or going. So give me this hill country that GOD promised me. You yourself heard the report, that the Anakim were there with their great fortress cities. If GOD goes with me, I will drive them out, just as GOD said. (Joshua 14:10–12 MSG)

Caleb was successful in driving out those giants—a claim he was not afraid to make the day Joshua gave him his inheritance … a claim he had not been afraid to make forty-five years earlier in the wilderness.

Be like Caleb. "Stick to your guns" by staying focused. Live to please the Lord and know that favor comes from him, not man. Stay diligent as you wait patiently on the Lord's perfect timing. Live in expectancy of God's blessings, and be a channel of his love to the world. Keep your priorities in order, and do not neglect your family as you serve the Lord. Say no to any distractions so that you can serve the Lord with your whole heart and enjoy your adventure with Jesus!

Key Treasure

Be like Caleb. "Stick to your guns" by staying focused.

DAY 6

Do not throw away your confidence; it will be richly rewarded. You need to persevere so that when you have done the will of God, you will receive what he has promised. For, "In just a little while, he who is coming will come and will not delay." And, "But my righteous one will live by faith. And I take no pleasure in the one who shrinks back." — *Hebrews 10:35–38*

Although the descendents of Judah and Joseph were active in pursuing their allotment, there were seven less-assertive tribes who had not yet received their inheritance (Joshua 18:1–2). Joshua called a meeting in the tabernacle at Shiloh with those passive tribes—Benjamin, Simeon, Zebulon, Issachar, Asher, Naphtali, and Dan. I can just imagine Joshua looking at them square in the eyes as he said, "How long will you wait before you begin to take possession of the land that the LORD, the God of your ancestors, has given you?" (Joshua 18:3).

Claim Your Inheritance!

When I first read those scriptures, I could almost hear the voice of Jesus saying the same words to me, "Aliene, how long will you wait to take possession of your inheritance?"

Jesus asks us the same question today. *How long will you wait to use those gifts I have given you? Why are you waiting until you are perfect, when it is through your weakness that I love to shine? What are you waiting for? How long will it take you to stop listening to other voices and follow the Holy Spirit's leading in your life?*

It was only a short time ago that God helped me see that for most of my life I have allowed someone other than Jesus to define my borders. When I was a little girl, I pretended that I was a teacher. Standing at the blackboard clutching a piece of chalk, I would teach my imaginary students. However, when I was in college, I did not major in teaching because certain people with influence in my life encouraged me to find another profession because "teaching kids these days is just not worth it." In high school, I wanted to be a cheerleader, but played competitive soccer because I felt people would be more pleased with me if I played a "real" sport. In my senior year of college, I co-hosted a talk show at a local cable station. At the end of my senior year, the station owner offered me a job. I turned him down because people told me that it did not pay enough.

As I started to seek Jesus, he set all that straight. Now I aim to serve him. I have finally recognized and fully accepted the gifts God has given me. I have sought him—and continue seeking him—to understand how he wants me to use those gifts. And I rely on him for the strength and wisdom to accomplish his purpose for my life. Every time I stand to teach God's Word and cheer others on to be *brave hearts* for Jesus, I feel the warmth of my heavenly Father's smile because I am finally taking possession of my purpose.

Spend Time with Him ...

Sometimes I believe the main reason we are waiting to take up our inheritance is that we get so busy with our routines that we accept life the way it is. We do not stop and take the time to ask Jesus where our boundaries are in the Promised Land. Today, let's spend some time sitting at his feet, praying, and seeking his face! Shut out all the distractions of the day. Get in God's presence; play worship music. Be led by the Spirit as you pray and seek the Lord. The next page is blank so you can journal as the Lord leads you. Spiritual gift surveys have their place, but ultimately it is Jesus who will give you your place in the Promised Land. Let's go together to Jesus, our Joshua and Great High Priest, and ask him to show us our allotment in the Promised Land.

Scriptures You May Want to Meditate On

Joshua 18:1–3 | John 21:15–25 | Romans 12:1–8 | 2 Timothy 1:3–7 | Hebrews 11 | John 14:11–14

Questions to Inspire Your Time Alone with the Lord

- When you were a child, what did you want to be when you grew up? What did you pretend to be?
- What do you enjoy doing?
- What things excite you?
- What do you dream of doing "someday soon"?
- What passions and desires exist in your heart?
- If you could change one thing about this world, what would it be?
- What are some of your God-given gifts and talents?

A Prayer to Get You Started

Jesus, I come to Shiloh to meet with you! You do not need to take a survey of me as Joshua did for the Israelites because you know everything about me. I am a divine creation. In your eyes, I am flawless. I confess I have tried to live in someone else's allotment and I am tired of allowing my envy to rob me of my own destiny. I am glad that because I am your child, the world and other people's opinions no longer define me. Peel back the layers and show me who you created me to be. Peel back the layers of voices in my life that have caused me to seek the approval of others. Today is a new day. I want to live and do what you have created me to do. Tell me what the first step should be, and I will no longer allow others to define me. Living outside my borders and trying to be someone else only makes me miserable. Show me who you created me to be. Speak to me today—I want you to be my life coach. I am tired of waiting, and I am ready to find my place in the Promised Land to bring you glory. Amen.

"What can I do for you, Jesus?"

Chapter 9

THE FAITHFULNESS AND PROMISES OF GOD

My nourish notes for Joshua 22-24

Day 1: Reveal

Meditate on the scriptures, prayerfully reading and reflecting on the verses. Mark the phrases, verses, or words that catch your attention. Journal and learn more as the Lord leads you.

Day 2: Respond

Respond to activate truth in your life. The **IMPACT** acronym provides questions to help you apply the Word. Sometimes you may not have an answer to all six questions.

Image of God to trust? *An attribute of God, Jesus, or the Holy Spirit to trust.*

Message to share? *A word of encouragement, truth, or a prayer to share with others.*

Promise to treasure? *A promise in the Bible to stand on by faith.*

Action to take? *A specific step God is calling you to take.*

Core authentic identity to embrace? *A truth about how God sees you to agree with in your heart.*

Transgression to confess or forgive? *A confession to receive healing, help, and restoration through Christ.*

Day 3: Renew

Carry God's Word with you during the week. Renew your mind daily by focusing on one word, verse, or truth that the Holy Spirit revealed through the Bible. Like an anchor that secures its vessel, renewing your mind with the truth brings security and focus, despite the waves you face during the day.

My Anchor of Truth:

NOURISH JOURNAL

Additional space to record any further thoughts God has shared with me.

DAY 4

*So that they may be brought to complete unity. Then the world will know
that you sent me and have loved them even as you have loved me.*
—John 17:23

It was time for the Transjordan tribes to return to the land they had claimed as their home—
outside of the Promised Land and east of the Jordan River. Back in the wilderness, these
tribes—the Reubenites, Gadites, and half of the tribe of Manasseh—had asked Moses if
they could settle just outside the borders of the Promised Land because they thought that
land was "suitable" for their livestock (Numbers 32:1). Although Moses pleaded with the
two and a half tribes to reconsider their decision, he granted their request with the stipula-
tion that they fight beside their brothers until the Promised Land was secure. Now that the
battles were over and the allotments made, Joshua blessed the Transjordan tribes and
sent them on their way.

As the homebound Transjordan tribes approached the border of Canaan, they decided
to build an altar to testify to future generations that, although they had settled outside of
the Promised Land, they were still a part of God's chosen people. The Transjordan tribes
wanted their grandchildren to have something tangible to prove they were Israelites. The
altar was grand in size and provided a witness to future Israelites.

Assumptions, Misunderstanding, and Strife

When the other Israeli tribes heard about the impressive altar, they assumed that the
Transjordan tribes had built it to worship other gods. They knew idolatry practiced by a
few could defile the entire nation and bring God's judgment—the destruction caused by
Achan's hidden sin was still fresh in their memory. How could they forget the plague that
took twenty-four thousand lives in the wilderness because the Israelites began to worship
the god Baal of Peor? (Numbers 25). And so the entire nation of Israel assembled in Shiloh
to go to war against their brothers in the Transjordan tribes in an effort to protect themselves and defend God.

The Israelites finally had peace in the Promised Land. Their enemies had been defeated.
Now division and miscommunication were stirring up strife within the family. One of Satan's
biggest tactics is to turn brothers and sisters in Christ against each other and create division among the family of believers.

Jesus Wants Us to Live in Unity

In Jesus Christ's last prayer before he died on the cross, he prayed for unity among believers (John 17:20–23). In his prayer, we see many things about the heart's desire of the Lord Jesus Christ. Jesus prayed that we would know that we were loved by the Father. Jesus prayed that we would be protected from the enemy. In his last request, Jesus prayed for unity. He knew that we would need each other for accountability, love, and support. Most importantly, our love for each other points people to Christ by bearing witness to the Father's unconditional love.

As much as Jesus wants us to love one another, Satan's strategy is to create division within the body of believers. Sometimes instead of living in unity, Christians can talk negatively about believers or churches or Christian organizations—even if these individuals and ministries have a heart for the gospel.

Instead of seeing believers who love and support one another, the world at times sees Christians attacking one another. Rumors based on hearsay are spread to others as truth. Instead of combating the world's attacks on God, Christians slander one another, resulting in strife instead of support among believers.

Satan would love to stir up trouble inside your local church body, your small group, or among your close Christian friends. Paul warned the Ephesians not to allow Satan to get a foothold through unsettled anger (Ephesians 4:25–27).

In your world, where is the enemy trying to get a foothold by causing division and strife? What is causing the division?

Avoiding Miscommunication

Misunderstanding usually creates tension. The Israelites living in the Promised Land misunderstood the motives of the Transjordan tribes. Because of what they *heard*, they thought the Transjordan tribes had built the altar to worship other gods (Joshua 22:11). Because of hearsay, a war almost broke out among God's family.

We must always remember to get clarification before we act. Just because we hear a rumor about a fellow Christian or a Christian organization does not mean that it's true. Jesus tells us that if we hear something that troubles us, we need to go the person and speak with him or her directly (Matthew 18:15). When we go right to the source of our trouble, the facts can be clarified. Gossiping or going to someone else actually makes the problem worse. When we choose that route, we go outside of God's will and nothing gets resolved. Gossip and slander solve nothing. First Peter 4:8 says, "Above all, love each other deeply, because love covers over a multitude of sins." Love does not keep a record of wrongs or stir up trouble (1 Corinthians 13:5).

I believe the Israelites had a legitimate reason for concern. However, their response was completely wrong and almost started a war. Have you ever witnessed how miscommunication can cause wars in the body of Christ?

Communicate with a Spirit of Restoration and Love

The Israelites sent Phinehas to speak to the Transjordan tribes. In the past, God had given Phinehas, a descendent of Aaron, a covenant of peace and priesthood for future generations because he had stopped the plague at Baal (Numbers 25). But now, instead of approaching the Transjordan tribes in a spirit of restoration and love, Phinehas lashed out in anger and judgment. He falsely accused them of breaking the law, acting in rebellion, participating in idolatry, and turning away from God (Joshua 22:15–20).

Phinehas actually means "mouth of brass."[1] Our mouths can get us into serious trouble if we don't think before we speak! God has not called us to judge but to restore. We may have the best of intentions, but if we speak without love, we will only sound like a noisy gong (1 Corinthians 13:1). Sometimes God *does* call us to restore our brothers and sisters in Christ, but even then it must be done in a loving way (Galatians 6:1–3; Matthew 7:1–6, 5:43–48).

Submitting to Leadership

The Transjordan tribes contributed to the strife as well. Following the leadership of Moses and accepting their inheritance in the Promised Land would have kept all the Israelites together. Instead, these Transjordan tribes chose to go their own way. Ultimately, that decision led to their building the altar that brought about such confusion. Without the need for an additional altar, the strife never would have happened in the first place.

When we follow church leadership, we are walking in line with the will of God. God appoints church leaders, and we make their responsibilities a joy rather than a burden when we follow their vision (Hebrews 13:17). Complaining about leadership in our church, our small group, or any other ministry in which we are involved does not promote unity. Neither does pulling away from the vision of the church by doing our own thing.

In your past, you may have experienced leadership that abused power. If so, trusting authority may be difficult for you. However, God never asks you to follow authority without question, but to follow *his* authority above all others. If those in authority over you abuse their power, you do not have to submit. If church leadership makes decisions that do not line up with God's ways, you are under no obligation to follow those in leadership.[2]

God wants us to be team players inside the church and empower leadership by following their direction. It is their role to seek God's direction and our role to come alongside and help. Sometimes in order to be a team player, we have to set our personal desires aside. The Transjordan tribes wanted to stay out of the Promised Land because they felt as if the land west of the Jordan would be better for their livestock, but God had planned even better things for them in the Promised Land. Although we cannot always see it, God's plan is always best.

Church leadership is a good thing. It gives us direction and protection. When we decide to be team players, the body of Christ is more effective in its mission. Support leadership even if you have different opinions on their decisions.

Ultimately, we must follow God, and there *are* times he calls us to part ways for very good reasons. John Wesley and Martin Luther are two examples of men who were called out of their churches to follow God. Parting can be a good thing. Paul and Barnabas parted ways because of a sharp disagreement. God brought good from the separation—two missionary teams were able to take the gospel to more areas than one could have (Acts 15:36–41).

Part of Love Is Letting Go

Moses, Joshua, and Phinehas let the Transjordan tribes go their own way to live outside of the Promised Land. God calls us to *encourage* one another, but we need to realize that we cannot *change* each other. Joshua told the Transjordan tribes to keep the law, love God, hold fast, and serve him.

Even if God calls us to speak the truth in love to individuals, we must then release them to make their own decisions. The Transjordan tribes wanted to be identified as God's children, but could not fully commit to Promised Land living. Part of love is letting go. You cannot manipulate anyone into the Promised Land. God has given all of us free will, and we cannot force anyone to live out their spiritual inheritance. The Pharisees tried to make people holy by requiring them to conform to a list of rules, but manipulation is not God's way.

Love—the Best Witness

Jesus said that love is our witness to the world that we are God's children. We do not have to agree with everyone, but we are called to love everyone. Sometimes love involves restoration, but more often than not, love calls us to bear with one another in love. God has given us the ministry of reconciliation so that we can reconcile others to God.

> From Ephesians 4:1–6 and 4:25–32, what are some things you can do to live a life of love within the body of Christ? What specific action will you take to help bring restoration to a broken fellowship?

Paul goes on to tell the Ephesians, "Follow God's example, therefore, as dearly loved children and walk in the way of love, just as Christ loved us and gave himself up for us as a fragrant offering and sacrifice to God" (Ephesians 5:1–2). God loves you unconditionally and now he is asking you to love your brothers and sisters in Christ—imperfections and all. Bear with one another in love that the church may bear the love of Christ to the world.

DAY 5

You know with all your heart and soul that not one of all the good promises the LORD your God gave you has failed. Every promise has been fulfilled; not one has failed.
—*Joshua 23:14*

Ruth Bell Graham was the wife of Billy Graham for sixty-five years. She raised five children while her husband traveled around the world to share the gospel of Jesus Christ. Ruth loved to study her Bible. She loved to write poetry. But most of all, Ruth loved the Lord. It was her great joy to serve him by serving others. In her later years as she reflected back on her life, Ruth told a reporter, "I've enjoyed growing old. There is so much to look forward to after this life, and there is so much to look back on, and the thing that stands out in my life, above everything else, is the promises of God that you have seen come true."[3] The promises and the faithfulness of God were two beacons that stood out to Ruth as she reflected on her life of service to the Lord.

Motivated by the Faithfulness and Goodness of God

Joshua, our mighty warrior who faithfully served the Lord all his life, recalled the promises and faithfulness of God as he reflected back over his journey. From slavery in Egypt, to wandering in the wilderness, and finally to resting in the Promised Land, Joshua saw God's faithfulness to the promise he had made to Father Abraham years before. In Joshua's old age, he gathered the Israelites together to say his good-byes. Knowing his life was coming to a close, Joshua shared from his heart about the promises and faithfulness of God in order to inspire the children of Israel to live for God.

Joshua's *brave heart* made a difference and yours will too. When we know God loves us, is for us, and will be faithful to keep all his promises, we are willing to cross any Jordan River or go anywhere he wants us to go. What else would inspire missionaries to risk their lives to share the gospel but the goodness of God? What else would motivate you to lose self and carry your cross but the faithfulness of God? What else would give you the courage to start that ministry stirring in your heart but the promises of God? What else would encourage you to follow Christ with a *brave heart* but the amazing love of God?

Joshua began his message by asking the Israelites to remember the faithfulness of God. He recalled, "The LORD has driven out before you great and powerful nations; to this day no one has been able to withstand you. One of you routs a thousand, because the LORD your God fights for you, just as he promised" (Joshua 23:9–10). In chapter 24, Joshua began with Abraham in telling the story of God's faithfulness to the nation of Israel throughout the years. Indeed, God was faithful to Israel, and he will be faithful to you, his child.

I think it is so important that we take time every now and then to look back in our own history and see the footprints of God in our lives. When we remember his faithfulness, we will follow our Great Shepherd anywhere he takes us.

Encouraged by the Promises of God

Joshua also encouraged the Israelites with the promises of God. With unyielding confidence in the Word, Joshua said, "Now I am about to go the way of all the earth. You know with all your heart and soul that not one of all the good promises the LORD your God gave you has failed. Every promise has been fulfilled; not one has failed" (Joshua 23:14).

God is faithful to his Word. He cannot go back on his Word because God cannot lie (Hebrews 6:18). The Bible is filled with thousands of promises from God. Take time to search through the Scriptures for those treasures and meditate on them day and night. Obedience to the promptings of the Holy Spirit requires reliance on the promises of God. Confidence to serve the Lord is born out of our trust in his unfailing promises.

Joshua warned the Israelites that if they did not keep the law (covenant) and turned to other gods, the Lord would bring disaster and drive them out of their inheritance. The responsibility to keep the covenant was on the Israelites. It is a different story altogether for us. As you step out with a *brave heart*, remember your Redeemer lives to keep the covenant for you. The good news is that his righteousness, his promises, and his faithfulness are yours because of your faith in the gospel message. Rest in his love, his promises, and your position as a child of God. Joshua's death separated him from the Israelites, but nothing will ever separate you from the love of Christ.

Serving Out of Love

Joshua challenged the Israelites to serve the Lord. Serving God would require sacrifice, but Joshua knew from experience that God is the only one worth giving our lives to. "Now fear the LORD and serve him with all faithfulness. Throw away the gods your ancestors worshiped beyond the Euphrates River and in Egypt, and serve the LORD. But if serving the LORD seems undesirable to you, then choose for yourselves this day whom you will serve, whether the gods your ancestors served beyond the Euphrates, or the gods of the Amorites, in whose land you are living. But as for me and my household, we will serve the LORD" (Joshua 24:14–15).

And this day and every day, God gives us a choice whether or not to serve him. The truth is that all of us will serve something or someone. Jesus went to the cross not out of duty or religious obligation, but out of love. If we serve God out of duty, we will grow weary … but if we choose to serve him out of love, we will follow him with passion. In the middle of our obedience when we realize that serving God means sacrifice and discomfort, it is God's love for us that will keep us carrying the cross to a lost world.

Meditate on the promises and the faithfulness of God, and you will fall in love with him over and over again. He loves you.

Empowered by the Holy Spirit

The Israelites responded with wholehearted promises to serve the Lord, but Joshua knew their hearts would be prone to wander away from God eventually. Even Joshua had made some mistakes along the way as he sought to serve the Lord with all of his heart. None of us have the ability to serve God on our own because of the sinful nature inside of us. When we attend church services and sing "I surrender," we can have the best of intentions, but we must realize that we cannot do it in our own strength. We must lean on God. Making a vow to serve God is noble, but it takes more than talk to walk the walk.

Joshua set up a rock as a witness so the Israelites would serve the Lord with all their hearts. Jesus Christ is our Rock, and today he lives within us through the Holy Spirit. "The Lord lives; blessed be my Rock, and exalted be God, the Rock of my salvation" (2 Samuel 22:47 AMPC). The Holy Spirit bears witness that we are God's children and empowers us to serve God. Following God wholeheartedly flows out of God's *love for us* through the grace of Jesus Christ and is empowered by the Holy Spirit.

Dedicated to Serving Him

You are a divine creation, empowered by the Holy Spirit to do great things for God. The promises of the new covenant and the faithfulness of God's grace give us the tools we need to dedicate our house to serve the Lord. Our house represents our bodies—God's temple for the Holy Spirit. David said, "Truly does not my house stand so with God? For He has made with me an everlasting covenant, ordered in all things, and sure. For will He not cause to prosper all my help and my desire?" (2 Samuel 23:5 AMPC).

My hope and prayer is that through this study you have learned a little more about your Promised Land—your new covenant position and identity in Christ. I pray that the real you, the beautiful designer's original, will stand up and begin to walk by faith in the calling God has given you. I pray that you will stop trying to fight your battles by using a formula … and start following Jesus. I pray that you will make the Great Shepherd your stronghold and trust him for everything. And most of all, I pray that you will know just how crazy God is about YOU, so that when you hear God's voice you will be brave and make a difference.

If God is calling you to do something that seems impossible—get radical and go for it. It is when we face our giants that the Lord fights for us and we see his faithfulness to the promises of the new covenant.

Choose to Step Out in Faith

Joshua's challenge to the Israelites is our challenge today. This day, you too must choose whom you will serve. You see, all of us are going to serve somebody or something. We cannot have two masters. Whoever or whatever we serve has captured our hearts. Open your heart to God and allow Jesus to capture your heart. You cannot do a thing to earn his love—just receive it. When you receive God's love for you, you can't help but fall in love with him and serve him the rest of your days. You have all the tools you need to follow him … your choice will make the difference. Choose to step out in faith and see God's faithfulness!

DAY 6

Blessed are those whose strength is in you,
whose hearts are set on pilgrimage.
—*Psalm 84:5*

When Joshua finished his farewell, he sent the Israelites back to their allotments in the Promised Land. Now that this Bible study has finished, where is Jesus sending you? If Bible study is just more head knowledge—that's religion. Allow the Word to make an impact in your life by going where Jesus wants you to go.

Today let's reflect on the study collectively. It is vital to rest, reflect, and remember. Pray and ask the Lord to help you remember those important milestones he does not want you to forget. And as you forge forward into your Promised Land, may you always be strong and courageous. Step out boldly, and be all God has created you to be by resting in his radical love for you.

1. How has your thinking about following God with your whole heart changed as a result of this study? What does it mean to have a brave heart?

_____

_____

_____

2. What attributes of God's character did you see this week? Out of all the illustrations of God's character you saw during your study of Joshua, what one is most dear to you and why?

_____

_____

_____

3. What is the greatest example of God's faithfulness to you that you have seen over the past nine weeks?

_____

_____

_____

4. Reflect over the commentary material. What did the Lord impress upon your heart the most and why?

_____

_____

_____

_____

5. Think back over the times you met with your small group. How were you able to see God's hand in putting your groups together? What did you learn from your time together?

_____

_____

_____

_____

6. Look back over your Nourish Notes and specifically at Day 3, "Renew." What Anchor of Truth created the greatest impact in your life?

_____

_____

_____

_____

"When Joshua had grown old, the LORD said to him, 'You are now very old, and there are still very large areas of land to be taken over'" (Joshua 13:1). In the Promised Land there will always be new areas to conquer, new battles to fight, new challenges to face. But glory to God, now that we know our position, our purpose, and our place as a child of God, we can set our hearts on a pilgrimage to follow Christ with courage and make a difference.

Although you have reached the end of the study, it is really only the beginning. I must admit I shed a few tears when I read about Joshua's death. He and I have grown pretty close over this past year. I believe Joshua lived his life with no regrets, because he spent his life following God and serving others. That is how I want to live mine. How about you, _brave heart_?

SOURCE NOTES

Chapter 1: BRAVE HEART

1. Jennifer S. Holland, *Unlikely Loves: 43 Heartwarming True Stories from the Animal Kingdom* (New York: Workman Publishing, 2013), 18.

2. Mother Teresa, "The Final Analysis" *The Wow Zone:* www.wowzone.com/final.htm.

Chapter 3: RESCUED

1. Jon Courson, *Jon Courson's Application Commentary New Testament*, (Nashville, Tennessee: Thomas Nelson, Inc., 2003), 1512.

2. Ibid., 1515.

3. Dictionary and word search for *yashab* (Strong's H3427). *Blue Letter Bible.* www.blue letterbible.org/lang/lexicon/lexicon.cfm?Strongs=H03427&t=KJV (accessed August 2008).

Chapter 4: THE NEW COVENANT

1. M.E. Arbaugh, *"God's Plan for Your Spirtual Health: How Covenants Are Established"*, Copyright 1998, www.peace4u.org/howcovenant.htm. (August 14, 2008).

2. Jon Courson, *Jon Courson's Application Commentary Old Testament Volume I Genesis–Job*, (Nashville, Tennessee: Thomas Nelson, Inc, 2005), 647.

3. Arbaugh, *"God's Plan for Your Spirtual Health: How Covenants Are Established"*

4. Ibid.

5. Ken Abraham, *Positive Holiness* (Old Tappan, New Jersey: Fleming H. Revell Company, 1988), 216.

6. Ibid.

7. Ibid., 94–95.

8. Joe Thompson, *Covenant Workshop*, 2007.

9. Ibid.

10. Neil Anderson, *The Bondage Breaker* (Eugene, Oregon: Harvest House Publishers, 2000), 46.

11. Dictionary and word search for *cherpah* (Strong's H2781). 1996–2008. *Blue Letter Bible.* www.blueletterbible.org/lang/lexicon/lexicon.cfm?Strongs=H02781&t=KJV (August 14, 2008).

12. Dictionary and word search for *Gilgal* (Strong's H1537). 1996–2008. *Blue Letter Bible.* www .blueletterbible.org/lang/lexicon/lexicon.cfm?Strongs=H01537&t=KJV (August 14, 2008).

Chapter 5: GOING THROUGH THE WALL

1. Dictionary and word search for *ochyrōma* (Strong's G3794). 1996–2008. *Blue Letter Bible.* www.blueletterbible.org/lang/lexicon/lexicon.cfm?Strongs=G3794&t=KJV (August 14, 2008).

Chapter 6: BLESSED ASSURANCE

1. Dictionary and word search for *chata'* (Strong's H2398). 1996–2008. *Blue Letter Bible*. www.blueletterbible.org/lang/lexicon/lexicon.cfm?Strongs=H02398&t=KJV (August 14, 2008).

2. Dr. Henry Cloud and Dr. John Townsend, *Boundaries* (Grand Rapids, Michigan: Zodervan, 1992), 99.

3. Ibid.

4. Warren W. Wiersbe, *The Bible Exposition Commentary Old Testament History* (Colorado Springs, CO: Cook Communications Ministries, 2003), 54.

5. Dictionary and word search for *metanoeō* (Strong's G3340). *Blue Letter Bible*. www.blueletterbible.org/lang/lexicon/lexicon.cfm?Strongs=G3340&t=KJV (August 2008).

6. Dictionary and word search for *quwm* (Strong's H6965). *Blue Letter Bible*. www.blueletterbible.org/lang/lexicon/lexicon.cfm?Strongs=H06965&t=KJV (August 2008).

Chapter 7: VICTORY!

1. www.facingthegiants.com (June 15, 2008).

2. Wiersbe, *The Bible Exposition Commentary Old Testament History*, 67.

3. Courson, *Jon Courson's Application Commentary Old Testament Volume I Genesis–Job*, 675.

4. Dictionary and word search for *shaqat* (Strong's H8252). *Blue Letter Bible*. www.blueletterbible.org/lang/lexicon/lexicon.cfm?Strongs=H08252&t=KJV (August 28, 2008).

5. Living Free Every Day, August 5, 2008, Living Free, Chattanooga, TN, www.LivingFree.org

Chapter 8: YOUR CALL, YOUR CHOICE

1. Dictionary and word search for *male* (Strong's H4390). *Blue Letter Bible*. www.blueletterbible.org/lang/lexicon/lexicon.cfm?Strongs=H4390&t=KJV (August 2009).

2. Jon Courson, *Jon Courson's Application Commentary New Testament*, (Nashville, Tennessee: Thomas Nelson, Inc., 2003), 1098.

3. Goodreads (©2009 Goodreads Inc), www.goodreads.com/quotessearch?q=family+mother+teresa (Accessed April, 2009.)

Chapter 9: THE FAITHFULNESS AND PROMISES OF GOD

1. Dictionary and word search for *Piynĕchac* (Strong's H06372). *Blue Letter Bible*. www.blueletterbible.org/lang/lexicon/lexicon.cfm?Strongs=H06372&t=KJV (August 15, 2008).

2. Nancy Alcorn, *Violated*, (Enumclaw, WA Wine Press Publishing, 2008), 35.

3. Billy Graham Evangelic Association, *Celebrating Her Life*, Multimedia Center, www.billygraham.org/mediaplayer.asp (June, 2008).

PRAYER REQUESTS

PRAYER REQUESTS